"Leading a team in turbulent and changing times is difficult. *The FUD Factor* is a refreshingly easy guide on how to do it well. This is a must-read for any manager."

—Zak Brown, CEO, McLaren Racing Limited

"Brendan has a unique ability to motivate and challenge his team to bring their A-games every day by intently listening, providing helpful encouragement, and being unabashedly transparent. His collaborative leadership approach is focused on getting to the right answer, not his answer."

—Olof Bergqvist, Managing Director, Bain Capital

"Brendan Keegan gives us a helpful recipe that applies to any organization, from start-ups to Fortune 500s. Get ready to take notes and shift the way you see things."

—Jonah Berger, Marketing Professor, Wharton School at the University of Pennsylvania; International Bestselling Author, *Contagious, Invisible Influence,* and *The Catalyst*

"My team and I had the great fortune of working directly with Brendan Keegan and, with this book, anyone can now have access to his insights, creativity, and wisdom. The world looks very different today, and leaders must be intentional, reflective, and, most importantly, fearless. Brendan provides the playbook that today's leaders—at any level—need more than ever."

—Paul LeBlanc, President,
Southern New Hampshire University

"Many people ascend to positions of leadership, usually by merit or proxy. Sometimes roles of leadership are given to people who deserve it but oftentimes to people who are not qualified for such ... and people can spot a fake pretty quick. If you are reading this book, I assume you have a keen interest in developing your leadership skills. I've had the unique pleasure of working directly with Brendan. I've observed, participated in, and benefitted from his mentorship and leadership. In his book, *The FUD Factor*, you too will experience practical, real-world guidance that, when applied, will give you a clear path to becoming a great leader."

—Tye Kuhlman, Account Director, Americas, Hemmersbach

"Through his book, Brendan Keegan helps readers awake the fearless leader within oneself by laying out how to overcome our unintentionally and unconsciously ingrained fear, uncertainty, and doubt. His thirty-year career journey serves as an open and honest backdrop to illustrate some of his groundbreaking lessons, which we can all learn from, especially in a postpandemic workplace. An absolute must-read if you too want to take your career to the next level by investing in yourself."

—Kirsten Rhodes, San Francisco Managing Principal, Deloitte LLP

"Brendan's insights on how to utilize fearlessness in your leadership journey are invaluable for any emerging leader, particularly when building a driven, top-notch team. I saw this firsthand when he was able to use these insights to build a fearless leadership team that took a small family-owned company through an unprecedented global pandemic and financial crisis and emerged on the other side bigger, better, and stronger as one of the most innovative players in the space."

—Kirk Hoffman, Managing Director, BNP Paribas

"It's not easy to lead a team during difficult times. But with *The FUD Factor*, author Brendan Keegan presents an easy-to-use guide to do just that. This should be required reading for every leader in today's ever-changing world."

—Maria Bailey, Managing Editor, Contributor Network, Entrepreneur.com

"When it comes to leadership, Brendan Keegan is the epitome of being a leader for everyone, young, old, and in-between. He uses confidence, knowledge, intelligence, and empathy to bring out the best in everyone. Embracing the message of this book will certainly enhance your own leadership qualities but also add value to other people's lives."

—Jon Goode, CEO, KBK Sports

"Brendan Keegan is a one-in-a-million leader who sets the gold standard. My company's transformation and ongoing success is heavily influenced by Brendan's leadership and advice. He has helped shape me as an owner, as a leader, and as a person."

—Andi Shaughnessy, Co-Owner and Co-CEO, ExpressIt Delivery

"Every time I read something penned by Brendan Keegan, I find myself energized to put my best foot forward as a leader. *The FUD Factor* is no exception. As he writes here: 'With the right foundation and tools, we can be ready for fear, uncertainty, and doubt when they do show up and prevent them from taking control.' Through insightful tips brought to life through personal stories, Keegan helps you become the fearless leader he knows—and now you know, too—that you can be."

—Yoni Stern, SVP Business Development, Systematic Inventive Thinking

"It's not often you come across a truly life-changing book. *The FUD Factor* provides the reader with actionable steps on the road to becoming the best version of yourself. Author Brendan Keegan makes the book very personable and shows his humility even after achieving so much success, which is another great hidden lesson throughout the book."

—Brian Cameron, Student-Athlete, Rutgers University

"Embracing the message of this timely book won't just add value to your business, it will add value to your life! Brendan Keegan brings fear, uncertainty, and doubt to life in a realistic and simplified way that exceeds any previous educational attempts."

—John Cail, SVP of Mobility, Merchants Fleet

"After attending several of Brendan's leadership trainings I was able to apply some of his methods to my position as school principal. The knowledge I have gained from Brendan has helped me build the competitive edge needed for success as a PK-8 school principal. In *The FUD Factor*, Keegan says it all here: 'We can choose to be the light others look to, the hope others rely on, the positive amongst the doom-sayers.' Brendan gave me the tools to recognize my strengths in order to develop myself as a leader. For this, I will be forever grateful."

—Cindy Clarke, Principal PK-8, Saint Christopher Academy

"Brendan Keegan is one of those rare leaders who not only understands and teaches theory but has person-ally put leadership into practice many times. Because of that, anyone who aspires to be a leader or to further their own leadership has more than something to gain from reading Brendan's work and implementing his systems. The knowledge I have gained from Brendan's fearless leadership training has been instrumental in my own career growth, and I have much gratitude for all that I have learned through Brendan's work."

—Amanda Rogers, Vice President, Marketing & Innovation, Merchants Fleet

"Adapting to our new normal postpandemic poses a challenge for today's business leaders. Guidance from Brendan arrives at a perfect time to ease you through this transition period and get you on the right path to lead your team to new heights. This is a must-read!"

—Chris Licata, President & CEO, Tecnica Group North America

"Brendan Keegan has produced a must-read story for anybody exploring leadership. Read this book, and learn from one of the finest."

—Chad Gundersen, Producer, *The Chosen*

"As a fellow CEO, I can't wait to devour *The FUD Factor* and use Brendan's knowledge and success to further my career as I learn to be a better leader."

—Jon Nelsen, CEO, PlayHardLookDope

"Brendan Keegan is an accomplished and successful CEO with a sincere desire to help others by sharing what he has learned. The strategies in *The FUD Factor* are universal, uniquely realistic, and provide a common-sense approach to embracing and understanding leadership. A must-read for those who want to add value to their personal and professional life."

—Jeanine Charlton, SVP, Chief Technology & Digital Officer, Merchants Fleet

"Brendan drives individuals to succeed! His strategy leads to success for those willing to put in the work. Once a person eliminates the fear of failure (or fear of success), there is not too much that can't be done!"

—Shaun Nelson, Executive Director, Nashua PAL

"Keegan's *The Fud Factor* forces us to hold a mirror to ourselves and consciously acknowledge the barriers to our success. By first understanding what it is that holds us back, we are better able to shift our mindset and unleash the confidence necessary to truly lead fearlessly!"

—John Geraci, Managing Partner, LGA, LLP

"Many people end up in leadership positions because they are good, if not great, at their work. Often, however, the person finds themselves in this new position with great instincts and strong knowledge but no formal background or training in leadership, creating fear, uncertainty, and doubt. Today's Fearless Leader cannot lead from a point of weakness but rather from a point of strength. *The FUD Factor* reads like a personal conversation between the author, Brendan Keegan, and the reader and is filled with practical examples and mission-minded wisdom. His professional coaching will help the emerging leader find their voice and inner courage to 'announce a certain outcome' during these most uncertain times."

—Linda Brodeur, President, Bishop Guertin High School

"The knowledge I have gained from Brendan Keegan has helped me build the competitive edge needed for success. In *The FUD Factor: Overcoming Fear, Uncertainty, and Doubt to Achieve the Impossible*, Brendan shows businesses of all sizes how to lead their company, and it certainly carries over to their personal life. Brendan's definition of leadership is uniquely well thought out and says it all here: 'Leadership is the willingness to accept responsibility to organize a group of people to achieve a common goal.'"

—Tom Boucher, CEO-Owner, Great NH Restaurants, Inc.

"Twenty-eight years ago, in 1994, I met Brendan Keegan at a wedding reception for one of my design staff. The moment that I met him, I knew that he was a really special young man. Within a minute of talking with him, I held onto his arm and told him 'I want you to meet my daughter!' Three years later Brendan married my daughter, Dana, and this year they celebrate their twenty-fifth wedding anniversary! They have gifted me with two wonderful grandchildren and another 'son' in Brendan! Through all these years, I have watched Brendan create, lead, and restructure businesses into profitable and super successful businesses, just as he has for Merchant Fleet. I call him 'My Business Genius!'"

"Brendan Keegan's spectacular career is an inspiration for all who aspire to lead others. In *The FUD Factor*, he shares hard-earned lessons in a clear manner that is both impactful and entertaining. His blend of personal experience and values combined with observations from other well-known leaders makes for interesting reading that will stay with you long after you've finished."

THE FUD FACTOR

THE
FUD
FACTOR

*Overcoming **Fear, Uncertainty
& Doubt** to Achieve the Impossible*

BRENDAN P. KEEGAN

Forbes | Books

Published by Forbes Books, Charleston, South Carolina.
Member of Advantage Media.

Forbes Books is a registered trademark, and the Forbes Books colophon is a trademark of Forbes Media, LLC.

Printed in the United States of America.

10 9 8 7 6 5 4 3 2 1

ISBN: 978-1-95588-446-4 (Hardcover)
ISBN: 978-8-88750-002-7 (eBook)

LCCN: 2022917372

Cover design by Matthew Morse.
Layout design by Matthew Morse.

This custom publication is intended to provide accurate information and the opinions of the author in regard to the subject matter covered. It is sold with the understanding that the publisher, Forbes Books, is not engaged in rendering legal, financial, or professional services of any kind. If legal advice or other expert assistance is required, the reader is advised to seek the services of a competent professional.

Since 1917, Forbes has remained steadfast in its mission to serve as the defining voice of entrepreneurial capitalism. Forbes Books, launched in 2016 through a partnership with Advantage Media, furthers that aim by helping business and thought leaders bring their stories, passion, and knowledge to the forefront in custom books. Opinions expressed by Forbes Books authors are their own. To be considered for publication, please visit **books.Forbes.com**.

To my mom, dad, sister, and brothers, who raised me to be fearless,
and to my wife, Dana, and my kids, Kaylie and Patrick,
who are my rocks.

Contents

Acknowledgments

When I think of my leadership journey and publishing this book from initial thought to bookshelf, there are so many people to thank. First, I would like to thank my mom and dad for always pushing me to be my best and instilling the confidence in me that my best could be anything I wanted it to be. Right behind my parents is my special-needs sister, Beth, whom I shared a room with from birth through ninth grade, when I finally mustered the fearlessness to ask for my own room in the basement. Next, I want to thank my brothers, Paul and Jay, for teaching me so many lessons in how to do things and oftentimes showing me the way not to do things as only older brothers can do.

This book would not be possible without the nearly thirty-year relationship with my best friend and wife, Dana. She was fearless on that first date and hasn't changed a bit since. When life has thrown us challenges, as it does, she stands strong with me. And at times when my strength is weakened, she is the rock I depend on. I also want to recognize my adventure-seeking daughter, Kaylie, who jumps from planes, swims with sharks, flies planes, and attends college on another continent—maybe I instilled a little too much fearlessness in her—and my son, Patrick, who is the kindest young man you will ever meet, until his fearlessness manifests itself on the athletic field.

Any success I have had in the business world is directly proportionate to the mentorship I have received from some of the smartest people I have ever met. I am forever grateful to Bill Dvoranchik, my first mentor, who worked hard to convince me that I needed to learn to play golf and gamble; so far, I am one for two. To Val Lyons, who saw something special in me and took a risk on a young kid with no experience but a lot of bold ideas. To John Harris, who polished my rough edges and ushered me into "executiveness," all the while displaying patience. To Gary B. Moore, who taught me risk-taking, leadership, and the fine art of Napa Valley Cabernet wines. And to Gary Fernandes, who showed me what a world-class executive was by simply affording me the opportunity to work with him and for refocusing me a time or two when I needed it.

Next, I want to thank the 250,000 women and men I have had the opportunity to lead into battle in the business world for placing your courage and faith in me to be your leader. I also want to thank the hundreds of thousands of subscribers to my newsletters and syndicated articles for inspiring me by your viewership, your comments, your likes, and your thumbs-up. A simple comment from someone ten thousand miles away makes me do what I do.

Last, I want to thank the team at Forbes Books for keeping me organized and on track and for always pushing me to be better.

Why Be?

Welcome to *The FUD Factor: Overcoming Fear, Uncertainty, and Doubt to Achieve the Impossible.* I am so thankful you have picked up this book, and I am genuinely excited to begin a conversation with you on perhaps the single greatest opportunity you will have during your lifetime. The opportunity to become a *Fearless Leader.* Yes, you can be fearless; we all can. It all starts with overcoming your ingrained FUD or fear, uncertainty, and doubt.

FUD is the fear the world puts on our shoulders throughout our life: "Be careful. You might hurt yourself" or "Nothing good has ever happened doing that." Next up is uncertainty: "I don't know if I would try that" or "That looks risky." And the third stop on the FUD train is doubt: "Go ahead and try out for the team. Just remember it is competitive, and you might not make it."

Why have we heard these types of statements in our life and oftentimes in our early life? Believe it or not, our loved ones were actually trying to protect us, but in reality, it was their FUD that was controlling their narrative. Because they didn't want to see us hurt if we didn't make the varsity cheerleading team, they were reminding us of how competitive it was in order to let us down gently. In reality they were instilling fear, uncertainty, and doubt and actually hurting our chances.

So how powerful is FUD? FUD is a weapon of mass destruction. Let's think politics for a minute. Have you ever heard "negative wins"? Listen to the next cycle of ads locally or nationally. "A vote for Smith is a vote against children." Is Smith really against children? Probably not, but the candidate running against Smith wants to instill the FUD factor into the race and to have you not vote for Smith because you are a young parent and you love your kids. And guess what was behind that statement? Research that young parents would determine the outcome of the election, so pushing the message that a candidate is bad for your kids is a pretty good approach to swing some votes.

When I first became a parent, the two things that surprised me the most were how little I knew and how often I sounded like my parents. And that brings me to generational FUD. Yes, FUD can be passed down unconsciously and unintentionally, like blue eyes or brown hair. If you are a parent, I bet you not only agree with those two things but also remember the times you sounded like your mom, dad, or childhood guardian.

Now the second half of overcoming your FUD on your path to fearlessness is becoming a leader. Throughout my thirty-year career journey, I have been fortunate to lead over 250,000 of the brightest women and men in over 150 countries. Investors have entrusted me with nearly $7 billion in capital to build and turn around their companies. And I have had the opportunity to grow revenue streams and develop over $100 billion of business with incredible clients globally. I have learned so many business and life lessons through the school of hard knocks, through successes and failures, and through hard work and teamwork. But the single biggest lesson I have ever learned I want to share with you personally. The difference between *good* teams and *great* teams, between *average* performance and *high* performance, and between *winning* and losing can be summed up in one single word: *leadership.*

My goal in writing this book is simple: help people see the Fearless Leader in themselves and accelerate their leadership journey. My purpose in life is to make Fearless Leadership possible for everyone by removing fear, uncertainty, and doubt. I have had the opportunity to lead six companies as president and/or chief executive officer. I have also built my own leadership consulting and training practice. These combined experiences enable me to bring real-life stories and proven processes to guide you on your Fearless Leadership journey.

> The difference between *good* teams and *great* teams, between *average* performance and *high* performance, and between *winning* and losing can be summed up in one single word: *leadership.*

What is the definition of *leadership?* There are hundreds, if not thousands, of definitions for *leadership*, and most people have their own opinion. This is how I define *leadership. Leadership* is the willingness to accept responsibility to organize a group of people to achieve a common goal. Let's break down the key components of that definition:

Willingness is having the desire to do something of your own free will. If you are performing an act simply because you were told to, you are demonstrating more management than leadership. That's not a bad thing; we have to do things we are told to, but let's not confuse the two concepts. Willingness is having or showing the ability to respond without being forced to and without delay.

To *accept* is having a favorable opinion or to take something upon yourself. It may even mean to put up with something that may be painful or challenging. But you accept it and move on. To accept is to confirm, ratify, concede, or confirm.

Responsibility is having to do something because of a prior agreement. It also means to be worthy of another's trust or confidence to get something done. Responsibility can represent both leadership and management. You can willingly be responsible, such as willingly voting in public elections. You can also unwillingly be responsible, such as taking the trash to the curb every week. Responsibility is an oath, a pledge, a promise, an arrangement, or a contract.

To *organize* is putting things, tasks, or people into a particular arrangement. For some, organizing is therapeutic, while for others it is a chore. Whichever one you represent, being able to organize is a critical element of leadership. To organize can mean laying things out, marshaling, systematizing, calculating, charting, designing, framing, strategizing, or mapping something out.

Group is usually a small number of people or things considered as a unit, such as a group of cars in a parking lot or a tour group coming to town. Groups come in many forms such as assemblies, congregations, gatherings, clans, cliques, fellowships, gangs, teams, task forces, schools, sects, or leagues.

People are human beings in general. Seriously, that's the initial definition in the online *Merriam-Webster's Dictionary*, funny but pretty accurate, especially considering this is a nonfiction, non-sci-fi book that may take exception to this definition. People are folks, a society, community, masses, populace, family, or the public.

To *achieve* is to obtain a goal through effort or to carry through to completion. They finally achieved making the varsity team. To achieve is to get, land, make, obtain, pull off, or accomplish something you set out to spend effort on.

Common is belonging or relating to the whole. It is also something that is done by a number of people as a group, for instance, working for the common good of the people. *Common* can mean synergistic, inclusionary, or symbiotic.

Goal is something one hopes or intends to accomplish. One of my main goals is to spread leadership. Goals are ambitions, aspirations, designs, dreams, ideas, ideals, and intentions.

We have defined *FUD* and what leadership is; now let's talk about the six reasons why leadership should matter to you.

Reason 1: The Leadership *Void*

In the United States alone, four million workers will retire this year, removing nearly fifteen million years of experience from the workforce. Think about it; that's ten thousand workers retiring every day at five o'clock. This mass exodus is creating the greatest leadership *void* in history.

Reason 2: The Greatest *Opportunity*

CEOs and executives are terrified of reason one. To run a successful business, whether a Fortune 100 company or a thriving small business, strong leaders are required. The leadership void has created the greatest *opportunity* of the past fifty years for individuals to accelerate their careers.

Reason 3: Leaders Are *Made*

Leaders are *made*, not born. Don't believe anyone who tells you otherwise. Leadership is not a birthright. Leadership is a *daily decision*. If you decide you want to be a leader, then you can become one.

Reason 4: Leadership Is the *Differentiator*

Everyone is looking for their differentiator, for something that makes them special and unique. Leadership is the *differentiator* you've been looking for. Once you have embraced the leader in you, many doors will open, and opportunities will come forward.

Reason 5: Leadership Is a *Gift*

There's no doubt leadership is hard work. But being a leader is the greatest *gift* you could ever give yourself. Once you have committed to leadership and driven a team to achieve something awesome, you will know what I mean. Leadership is a gift that will allow you to pursue your dreams and to create dreams for others as well.

Reason 6: The *Multiplier* Effect

We all wish we could multiply time, but we can't. However, we can *multiply* our impact every day by being a leader. When you instill and inspire leadership in others, you are creating multiple waves of success that ripple out and impact the greater world. Accepting the role of a leader truly allows you to multiply your impact and success.

Welcome to your Fearless Leadership journey and overcoming the FUD factor.

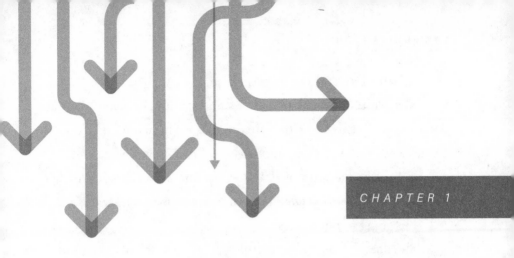

CHAPTER 1

Be Fearless

You were born *fearless*. We all were. As kids we jumped on skateboards without helmets, got behind the wheel of the neighborhood go-kart without pause, rode in back seats without seat belts, and ran through puddles in the rain just because. In each of those moments, we lived without fear, uncertainty, or doubt. We lived in the moment, and that moment was truly fearless.

As time marched on, fear marched in. "Put a helmet on."

"You're going to catch a cold."

"That's not safe for you to do."

"You're going to hurt yourself." Those were simple words that were meant to protect us and said ever so lovingly. But the unintended consequence was that unconscious fear began to take root, effectively the birth of *fear*.

As we grew into our adolescent years, fear shifted to *uncertainty*. This played out through thousands of what-if scenarios in our heads. "What if I don't make the team?"

"What if I don't do well on the test?"

"What if they don't like me?" As normal human beings, we like certainty; we like to know the outcome. As we have traveled through life, uncertainty grew more pervasive, and fear grew with it.

Each of us has stumbled at some point in our lives, and that stumble gave birth to *doubt*. "I'm not going to make the team."

"I'm going to fail the test."

"She doesn't like me." One thing I have learned about doubt is this—no one is immune to it. The world's greatest leaders, artists, and athletes talk about early and ongoing doubts, even when they have reached the height of success.

Nobel laureate Maya Angelou once remarked, "I have written eleven books, but each time I think, 'uh oh, they're going to find out now. I've run a game on everybody, and they're going to find me out.'"[1]

Pres. Bill Clinton admitted to having a lot of self-doubt when he was young. As he put it, "I was always holding myself to a very high standard of failing, never as good as I wanted to be as a person, as a student, as anything, as a musician." While he believes some self-doubt is healthy, "If it's too strong in your life, it can paralyze you."[2] He credits his mother for helping him deal with doubt. Her life was hard, but she got up every morning, put a smile on her face, and went out and did her best. She taught him that obstacles were as much a part of life as opportunity and that we all have to keep moving forward.

---

1   Dr. Margie Warrell, "Afraid of Being 'Found Out?' How to Overcome Imposter Syndrome," Forbes, April 3, 2014, https://www.forbes.com/sites/margiewarrell/2014/04/03/impostor-syndrome/?sh=68191d2b48a9.

2   Mentoring Month, "President Bill Clinton – On Mentoring Interview & Self-Doubt," YouTube, October 18, 2013, https://www.youtube.com/watch?v=uGE5Y3fJkfY.

If we allow fear, uncertainty, and doubt to settle into our beings, then surely thoughts of *failure* will paralyze us next. "I'm not going to try out."

"I'm going to drop that class."

"I don't like him anymore." The fear of failure manifests itself as not wanting to try. Remember the words spoken to us as a kid to protect us from ourselves? Well now, we have moved onto self-preservation mode through self-talk. Arianna Huffington, president and editor in chief of the Huffington Post, referred to this self-talk as her obnoxious roommate. "I wish someone would invent a tape recorder that we could attach to our brains to record everything we tell ourselves. We would realize how important it is to stop this negative self-talk and push back against our obnoxious roommate with a dose of wisdom."[3]

By employing thoughts of failure, we are effectively insulating ourselves from being hurt, disappointed, or rejected. This is normal and ordinary; the key is to not allow it to rule our lives.

You can conquer fear, thrive in uncertainty, and shut the door to doubt. You can truly be *fearless*. Let's find out how.

Fear

"Dad, don't freak out, but I fell off my board. Looks like I got a concussion."

"What happened? Are you all right?" I ask, trying so hard not to freak out.

---

3   Vivian Giang, "8 Female Leaders on How to Overcome What's Holding Women Back," Fast Company, September 10, 2014, https://www.fastcompany.com/3035478/8-successful-women-leaders-on-how-to-overcome-whats-holding-women-back.

"You know that hill on campus that curves to the left and leads to my dorm? Well, I picked up a little too much speed, and …"

I'm really trying to listen, but all I want to do is ask, "Did you go to the infirmary? Were you wearing your helmet? Are you sure you have a concussion? If you hadn't traded in the safe board I got you for this faster one …" And that's exactly what I do as soon as Kaylie takes a breath.

Kaylie sighs on the other end of the phone. "Dad, I fell. I'm fine. It's no big deal."

She's right, of course. She isn't broken, and thankfully, in this moment she is immune to my unintentional attempts to create fear in her.

Once I recognized my own fear for my daughter's safety, I was better able to stop letting my fears become her fears. Did I want to run out and buy every piece of protective equipment there was and insist that she wear it? Absolutely—but I didn't. I managed my own fears so that I wouldn't create a bubble of fear in Kaylie that would hold her back. By recognizing our fears, we can begin to learn how to manage them.

Fear Is Real

I would be a liar if I told you fear doesn't exist—it does. Understanding why it exists and how it originates can help us better navigate it. As parents, we model, consciously and unconsciously, whether we should or shouldn't fear something, and our children pick up on that. My reflexive response to my daughter falling off her board modeled fear for all the things that *could have* happened. If I had continued down that path, I may have been successful, resulting in Kaylie being afraid to continue boarding or taking other risks. That's rarely our intention.

"Contrary to popular belief, fear isn't something we're born with, it's something we develop over time. In fact, babies don't demonstrate fear for the first time until around eight to twelve months of age, and it's usually in response to new people or events, particularly strangers … babies are more likely to judge the stranger to be threatening when they're not in a safe space."[4] In other words it's not just the person, animal, or thing that creates fear on its own but context also plays a role.

In her article "How We Learn to Be Afraid," LoBue goes on to explain that our fears are learned throughout our lives primarily through conditioning or a negative experience. The highly common fear of spiders and snakes is a great example. So common are these two fears that some researchers believe they are innate and evolved to protect us from dangerous predators. However, research by LoBue and colleagues indicates that our fear of snakes and spiders is learned through our environment. They found that preschool-aged children who viewed moving snakes and spiders on a touchscreen will reach for them and try to pick them up. They're curious but not fearful. And it's not just videos of snakes and spiders that they are willing to engage with. When presented with options to interact with live snakes, spiders, and hamsters, children eighteen months to three years will play just as eagerly with the snakes and spiders as they will with cute, little, furry hamsters.

So why do so many of us harbor this irrational fear of snakes and spiders? Have you ever seen an evil symbol of a hamster or a movie that depicted hamsters as aggressive, dangerous animals? Probably not. But the list of inherently evil and dangerous spider and snake symbols

---

4   Vanessa LoBue, PhD, "How We Learn to Be Afraid," Psychology Today, October 2020, accessed February 2, 2022, https://www.psychologytoday.com/us/blog/the-baby-scientist/202010/how-we-learn-be-afraid.

and stories that we are exposed to over our lifetime is endless. We have *learned* to cuddle hamsters and fear spiders and snakes.

The good news is if we can learn what to fear, we can unlearn it too.

Fear Is Only as Strong as We Allow It to Be

You can own your fear and beat it! I have had two major fears in life, a fear of my dad passing away and a deathly fear of heights. Trust me, both of these fears are clear and present; just ask my family. If my dad passed, I feared for my mom and my special-needs sister. How would they manage without my dad around? Mom has never driven a car, so how would they get groceries or visit the doctor? To manage that fear, my family and I decided that we would move back to New Hampshire and take care of them. That action replaced my fear with a true sense of calm; I knew my mom and sister would be taken care of. The fear was confronted, owned if you will, and subsequently beat.

> If we can learn what to fear, we can unlearn it too.

Now my fear of heights has not been beaten, and honestly, I don't think it ever will. But I also won't let it stop me from experiencing life. I know my limits and try to push myself beyond them whenever possible. When my wife was eight months pregnant, we decided to walk across the Golden Gate Bridge in San Francisco. That's no small feat for someone as afraid of heights as I am, but I figured that if she could do it a month before her due date, then so could I. My wife made it all the way over and back, and I am proud to say I made it halfway over and slithered back. I confronted my fear and pushed myself farther than I'd gone before, and the next time, I'll push myself a little more, each time building up my courage.

Fear will build momentum *if you let it.* Fight it inch by inch, day by day, and instance by instance, and you will strengthen your own power to shut it down.

Uncertainty

"John, I want you to start two new businesses in the next thirty days, and it's OK if one of them fails."

That statement created waves of uncertainty for John, a member of my leadership team. "Well, I have to make sure they'll make money before I can start them," he said.

"I'm not asking you to make money," I said. "I'm asking you to start two new businesses. There's a market for truck rental. Let's start with that."

Two weeks later I checked in with John to see if the new fleet of rental trucks was on their way. "I'm going to order fifty to get us started," he said. "We don't have the plan fully worked out yet, and I don't want to order more than we can handle. We'll increase gradually." John was still struggling with the uncertainty of the business failing and the fallout from that, even though I had given him permission for one of them to fail.

I knew he wouldn't get over his uncertainty quick enough on his own to capture the market that was ready right now. I needed to create what I call a forcing mechanism. I ordered five hundred trucks and told John, "You're in the truck rental business now. The trucks will be here in three months, so you have three months before you have to start renting."

To give a little more context to John's uncertainty, I had just come on board as CEO of Merchants Fleet, a company John had been with for thirty years. I don't want to suggest that all of his uncertainties were unfounded. He didn't know me or my leadership style, and to top it off, I had no previous experience in the fleet industry (more on that later). So how could he be certain that (1) I knew what I was talking about, and (2) I wouldn't fire him if he did fail one of the new businesses? He couldn't. That uncertainty created a fear that paralyzed John from taking action. John's inaction created a greater chance of failure than taking the uncertain risk. Think about that. If John had chosen not to move forward with the business, he was 100 percent guaranteed to fail and potentially lose his job, yet he was still reluctant to pull the trigger and take the risk. Doubts, uncertainties, and risks can be powerful. They can also be overcome.

Uncertainty breeds uncomfortableness. When we know an outcome is certain, we feel comfortable and even confident. But as the percentages slip from certain to uncertain, we become anxious, restless, and irritable. Over the course of our lives, we will be put into thousands of uncertain situations, so are we really going to let ourselves live with anxiety and restlessness, or are we going to accept uncertainty and learn to embrace it? Reflect on situations in your life when the cards have been stacked against you but you overcame the odds and won. Channel that reflection in times of uncertainty.

Outcomes Beat Uncertainty

There is no place to hide in F1 racing. For all involved it's like a livestream to the world 24/7. On race day cameras are in everyone's face. Off the racetrack there are continuous requests for interviews, which are videotaped and sent out to the unforgiving world of social media, and now Netflix has made it a reality TV show. So who in their right mind would want to head up a world-renowned racing team—a team that hadn't won in over seven years? Enter Zak Brown.

Former professional racer and successful entrepreneur, Zak Brown joined McLaren Racing at the end of 2016 as executive director of McLaren Technology Group and then took the helm as CEO in April of 2018. He had his work cut out for him. The company had been mired in management controversy that resulted in far more losses than wins on the racetrack and a serious downgrade in their reputation. The critics didn't take long to emerge, complaining that Brown was "too much like a teenager in charge of the train set" and "like a kid in the candy store" and "talks too much." Brown was unfazed, happy to be the proverbial kid in the candy store.

Then there's the feeling of some in the industry that Alonso, world champion and McLaren's star driver, was the one really calling the shots for McLaren Racing. Cue flashing cameras. Once again Brown remained unfazed.

As a turnaround CEO and a huge sports fan, I eagerly followed Zak Brown's evolution as McLaren CEO. What I have admired most is his unwavering confidence that McLaren could and would regain its position at the top of the Constructors' Cup and, perhaps more importantly, his ability to transfer that confidence to every member of the McLaren team, steadily easing their fear, uncertainty, and doubt. Here's how he has done it.

I joined in the worst year in the history of McLaren. Morale was down. Trust was down. My role had been a bit of a revolving door over the previous six years. As you can imagine, the environment I was coming into was very unsettled, and so I needed to understand how we got to where we were. It became clear to me that the absence of strong, consistent leadership was the downfall that bred a lack of transparency and communication that led to lack of trust.

The first thing I needed to do was transform my leadership team into one filled with excellent, transparent communicators, so we could begin to rebuild that trust. In the beginning I think I overcommunicated, but it was critical that every member of the team knew where we were, where we were going, and how we were going to get there. I pushed the leadership team to be transparent even when the truth was hard to hear. Everyone regains their trust at different times and in different ways, so it was important that the leadership team was disciplined in our approach and continually walked the walk and talked the talk.

Next, I set more numeric goals and objectives that gave everyone the benefit of the doubt. There was such an ingrained lack of trust and culture of fear that when mistakes were made, the assumption was that it had been done with malicious intent, and placing blame was a priority. I set out to change that mindset by communicating to everyone that mistakes will be made; let's give everyone the benefit of the doubt that their mistakes are just that, mistakes, because in the end, we're all in this together. I needed to get everyone to realize that all thousand of us are working behind the same two race cars and that we are going to win or lose together.

Gradually, I could see trust being reestablished. People began communicating back to me. Now when I went into a room and spoke to a group, when I asked if there were any questions, hands started to be raised. People began emailing me, and my door started getting knocked on. That's when the shift in culture really gathered momentum.

Communication is key, and it can be challenging in a large organization. There are times when I speak to the company as a whole, but those settings make it hard to connect on a personal level. I've created opportunities to communicate in more intimate group settings, and one way we do that is through what we call Chatham House rules. Once a week up to twenty people in the organization can sign up to participate in the meeting with me where they are encouraged to freely discuss any concerns or suggestions.

Communicating at this level can help flip negative experiences that have resulted from a simple oversight. At McLaren we have a gym for employees. In one of our Chatham House rule discussions, someone on the night shift complained that they didn't have access to the gym because they worked 7:00 p.m. to 5:00 a.m., and the gym was only open from 9:00 a.m. to 6:00 p.m. Turns out it was just an oversight that no one on the day shift had thought of. I looked into the cost of health and safety to have the gym open twenty-four hours a day, and now our night shift has the same access as everyone else. A small thing, but it had created negativity in the night shift crew, feeling like no one cared about or listened to them—it created a separation. That conversation and subsequent solution couldn't have happened without trust and open communication.

Transparency, communication, and trust are intertwined, and when you consistently practice transparency and engage in active communication, you build the trust needed to unite your team toward a common goal.

Brown's Fearless Leadership is beginning to produce winning outcomes that the organization hasn't seen since 2012:

- 2019: McLaren reestablishes themselves as clear "best of the rest" behind the big three teams. Third place in Brazil marks their first podium in five years.
- 2020: McLaren is quick and consistent, beating their upper-midfield rivals to P3 in the standings, with Carlos Sainz and Lando Norris both scoring podium finishes.
- 2021: McLaren records their first win since 2012, with Daniel Ricciardo and Lando Norris taking the year's only one-two result by any team at Monza.[5]

Commit to Confidence

Like Brown I have been the executive parachuting into troubled companies to fix them. Part of my responsibility was to remove the employees' fears and feelings of uncertainty so they could focus on better serving our clients. I took that responsibility seriously and committed 100 percent to all the employees so we would turn the

---

5   "McLaren - Year by Year," Formula 1, accessed April 1, 2022, https://www.formula1.com/en/teams/McLaren/Year_by_Year.html.

company around and win. Fundamentally, I was announcing a certain outcome. Now what I couldn't tell them on day one was how. That didn't matter, however, because the emphasis was on removing uncertainty and replacing it with confidence.

In life when confronted with uncertainty, follow these three steps:

- First, focus on the outcome you want. Research has proved you are 50 percent more likely to achieve a focused outcome.
- Next, determine how you will achieve that outcome and begin to build the individual actions that will get you to that result.
- Third, commit to do what it takes to win.

By committing your mental energy to completing the daily actions with a clear picture of the desired outcome, you illuminate your own path to success.

Doubt

The difference between winning and losing is most often not quitting.

—WALT DISNEY

If anyone had a reason to give into doubt and call it a day, it's Walt Disney. His initial business failures left him in tremendous debt, but his imagination and motivation were undeterred. He continued to pursue film animation, and the idea for Mickey Mouse was born. Mickey was an overnight success, right? Not so fast. Mickey Mouse was an imaginative sketch that required funds to bring it to film, funds that Disney did not have, so off he went to get a loan from the bank. Doubting Disney and Mickey's chance of success, the first bank denied his loan. More than three hundred other banks followed suit—three hundred![6]

Walt Disney pushed past all the doubters and brought Mickey to the screen, and well, we all know how that turned out.

The Evil Twin of Uncertainty

On our path of fear, uncertainty is the first to knock on our door. If we let it in, doubt will soon follow. Just as we discovered with fear, uncertainty and doubt develop from conditioning and negative experiences. If his past business experience was any indication, Disney couldn't be certain Mickey would be a success and neither could the banks. While Disney was willing to push past his uncertainties, those he asked to fund him turned the uncertainties of "This venture might not be successful" to "No way is this mouse going to make it." Disney's resiliency to overcome his uncertainties, push past his doubts, and keep knocking on doors finally led to a banker who didn't allow his own doubt to take hold and was willing to take the risk.

Not all of our doubts require Disney-sized perseverance or are make-or-break success scenarios. But those little thoughts of "How can this go wrong? What if this doesn't work?" that pop in our head can sow the seeds of doubt that keep us from moving forward. For most of us, those triggering thoughts occur when we are faced with change by choice (my family and I chose to move close to my parents) or force (after thirty years of doing things the same way, John had to find a way to overcome his perceived need that everything had to be perfectly aligned before he could begin).

---

6   Eudie Pak, "Walt Disney's Rocky Road to Success," Biography, updated June 17, 2020, accessed February 13, 2022, https://www.biography.com/news/walt-disney-failures.

You accept a job offer, and as you're handing in your resignation to your current boss, you think, "I'm successful here. They like me. I shouldn't leave."

Your son's getting on the school bus for the first time, and you think, "He's not going to get on the right bus home." These fleeting thoughts of doubt in uncertain situations are normal, and they even happen in situations in which we have already experienced success.

You're about to give a presentation, something you've done dozens of times, and just before you walk to the podium, you think, "This is the time I'm going to freeze and forget what to say. I just know it." This doubt in continued success is something I frequently witness through my work with velocityHUB, a company I founded that provides training programs, high-value consulting, and targeted executive coaching to many of the world's leading companies. It never fails to surprise me when, despite their success, executives and entrepreneurs doubt their ability to repeat that success. I could meet with them in January, on the heels of a tremendously successful year, yet at the top of their minds is doubt that they can do it again this year. I'd come in pumped for them about their success and their opportunity to not just repeat it but also exceed it, and their response would be, "That was last year. We don't know if that's going to happen again this year."

"Last year you had a great year, which was better than the year before, right?" I'd ask.

They'd nod yes, and I would say, "Why don't you think this year is going to be better?"

Immediately, they'd spout off a list of all the what-ifs that could cause them to fail. "What if we lose our top client?" they'd ask.

"How are you doing with them now?" I'd reply.

"Oh, we're doing great with them. They're extremely happy with us." And on it would go. They were more in touch with the reasons why they *couldn't* be successful than the reasons why they could. I walked through this process with them, helping them focus on all the ways and whys their success would continue, and by the end of the hour, the team would shift from doubting their success to "This is going to be our best year ever!"

> Doubt is a part of life; it's how we manage it that matters.

Doubt is a part of life; it's how we manage it that matters.

Beat Doubt with Mental Toughness

Managing doubt requires resilience and mental strength. Doubt doesn't send us a calendar notice of when it is going to pop up, so we need to be ready for it by building our mental strength and resilience daily. Here are a few ideas that work for me.

Exercise

Yes, once you get past the initial curve of conditioning, exercise can be one of the most amazing mental strength builders. A lot of people are group exercisers, and I am super envious of them. For me, I like to be alone, get a sweat on, and reflect on how I am going to win the day. You'll have your greatest success at sticking to it if you choose the type of exercise that you most enjoy and are motivated to do.

Reading

Spend quality time reading, reflecting, and simply escaping the chaos of the day.

Prayer or Meditation

Getting a good prayer in or a few moments of mindful meditation can be an amazing doubt reliever and leave you feeling spiritually nourished.

Nutrition

Getting good and healthy nutrients into your body to fuel your energy level is one of the most important things you can do to stay strong.

Family

Stepping away from the grind and focusing on what may be most important to you allows you to reset your priorities and see things more clearly.

Gratitude

Practicing gratitude and staying positive in the moment is a de-stressor and fills our head with good vibes.

Sleep

We all need our rest, especially in the most challenging of times, and that should be seven to eight hours a night.

Whatever tools you tap into to build your resilience and mental strength, consistency is key. Who knows? Maybe you'll even vanquish some doubts. Michael Jordan did.

"Before every game, you'd see MJ alone, head down, chewing his gum, having a private conversation with himself. He felt the same nerves you might feel before you're about to face a challenge. But he never doubted that he would perform at his best," said Tim Grover, Jordan's longtime coach.[7]

---

7   Jade Scipioni, "Traits That Help You Win at Anything, according to Michael Jordan's Trainer," CNBC Make It, May 13, 2021, accessed February 14, 2022, https://www.cnbc.com/2021/05/13/michael-jordans-trainer-principles-for-winning.html.

When asked if he ever doubted his abilities on the court, Jordan's response was, "Never." Why? "I've never been afraid, because I'm confident in my skills. I've put in the hard work."[8]

He's vanquished his doubts about his ability on the court, allowing him to fearlessly take shot after shot. So what *does* Jordan fear? Snakes!

With the right foundation and tools, we can be ready for fear, uncertainty, and doubt when they do show up and prevent them from taking control.

Fear of Failure

"OK, Houston, we've had a problem here." Jack Swigert spoke those words on April 13, 1970. As if attempting to visit the moon wasn't difficult enough, Swigert and the rest of the crew of Apollo 13 had a serious mechanical failure on their hands. It's safe to assume that everyone on the other end of that radio transmission, working from inside NASA's command center on the ground, felt a knot rise up in their stomach.

This wasn't just the fear of any failure. It was the failure of years of hard work, millions of dollars, and most importantly bringing the three astronauts home safely. Of course, we now know that no one involved let fear stop them. Instead of giving up or being paralyzed by doubt, they channeled their fear into the greatest creative problem-solving exercise to ever take place, devising and engineering solutions for a crisis happening over two hundred thousand miles above Earth's surface.

While most of us haven't experienced an Apollo 13–level failure, we've all experienced the fear of failure at some point in our lives, but

---

8   "The Mind of Michael Jordan-Confidence," September 13, 2020, accessed February 14, 2022, https://www.youtube.com/watch?v=NauAxHkqAyA.

that doesn't mean we all look at it the same way. Some of us associate it with the consequences of failing. We stress that we won't get the job we want or that we won't measure up to someone's expectations or our own.

But there's another way to look at the fear of failure and the stress and anxiety that inevitably come with it. We can remember that these feelings have been the source of some of the world's most impressive achievements, as well as a fundamental factor in the ability of humans to thrive both individually and collectively. We can choose to see the fear of failure as an opportunity.

Motivated by Fear of Failure

Our technology division was in trouble. Our biggest client served us with a ninety-day cure notice or termination, and the division just lost money for the third month in a row. That was the backdrop as I walked across our corporate campus as the new technology division leader. Your first thought might be, "Who would want that role?" The answer for me was simple: I did because amazing things can happen when our backs are up against the wall.

Failure was imminent. In my first meeting with the technology leadership team, I stated I was here to fix the problem, and we had ninety days to do it. As we went around the room, with each functional leader taking their turn for open discussion, I began to size up the situation. When we got to the fifth leader who was in charge of field operations, I got hit with "Hey, Brendan, what do you know about running a field services technology division?"

"Fair question," I said. "I have no experience running a field services technology company. I equally don't have experience getting served a ninety-day cure notice. I also don't have experience losing money three months in a row. And lastly, I have no plans to gain that experience with all of you. What I do have is experience turning companies and divisions around. We will cure our service within ninety days, and we will make money within sixty days. What I need to know is who is committed to winning, and if you have any doubt we will win, now is your time to speak up."

rightSIDE Up

As a turnaround executive for over a decade, I developed a methodology for fixing distressed companies. I named it rightSIDE up. It requires you to look at *everything* from the right side, not the wrong side. The wrong side doesn't take much looking; it's there, and for some psychological reason, people really like to talk about it.

"Our market has dried up, our sales team has lost their focus, there is too much pressure on pricing, and overseas markets are hurting us." I am not going to tell you any of those reasons aren't true. I simply don't know. But what I do know is if you focus on them, they will become your reality. Turn all of those words on the right side and focus on moving up.

"We need to identify a new market, we need to better train our sales teams, we need to become more efficient so we can sell our product for 5 percent less, and we need to compete globally." Winning in challenging times, like during a global pandemic, starts with how you frame your situation. Framing it negatively is wrong. Framing it positively is the *rightSIDE up*.

Open discussion concluded, we got to work creating a series of work streams focused on understanding the full situation: client, product/service, operations, people, and financial. Each work stream was given clear direction and twenty-four hours to come back with the top five challenges in order of magnitude. I always take this approach because it is the easiest assignment for everybody to do, the problems were easy to spot, and people would be willing to talk about them.

The next day we discussed every team's list as a group, and then each team was given another twenty-four hours to solve one of the challenges that was selected by the group based on hearing all of them collectively. At the end of this process, we determined that each technician was doing 2.3 transactions a day, and to become profitable, we needed to do 3.0 transactions a day. We also determined that 18 percent of our technicians were providing really poor service, which drew our overall performance down with our biggest client. On my fourth day, we held a town hall, and I outlined our rightSIDE up plan.

Starting Monday each technician would complete 3.0 transactions or more per day at an 80 percent performance score or greater. Not everyone on the team was convinced; some said it couldn't be done. We kicked off the town hall, and I had four PowerPoint slides as the backdrop:

Slide 1: We are in *trouble*.

I spoke authentically, transparently, and with empathy and explained our service issues and our profitability.

Slide 2: 3.0 transactions every day

I explained that we were losing money because we weren't getting enough billable work done each day and that starting Monday each technician would complete 3.0 transactions or more per day. I didn't pass judgment; I simply said it as factual and pragmatic.

Slide 3: 80 percent performance every day

I outlined the need to perform at 80 percent or better on every call by every technician every day, again a simple message with no room for ambiguity.

Slide 4: Sixty-day happy hour

I had a picture of a cocktail and told them in sixty days we were having a company happy hour. If we didn't succeed, we would be toasting and saying our goodbyes as the company would no longer exist. If we won and succeeded, we would be toasting to a brave, new future. I told the team that I was planning on a brave, new future.

Our technicians did it! They ramped up to 3.2 transactions per day and pushed our service levels up to 80 percent or higher. We made money, and our client was healthy again. But why were our technicians able to do in sixty days what they were unable to do for years? We turned the fear of failure rightSIDE up and to our advantage. We used it as our rallying cry. The stakes were high, and there was little room for fear, uncertainty, or doubt. Each person knew what they had to do. They just had to do it.

Now keep in mind, as the leader, I never fixed a hard drive, a motherboard, or a blown circuit board. I didn't perform a single transaction nor get any type of score. What I did do was channel my fearlessness to remove fear, uncertainty, and doubt in others.

Being Fearless

The bell rings; they shrug on their gear, jump in their truck, and race as fast as they can to the burning building that they will then run into, not knowing what's on the other side. Is it a grease fire, meth house, or a gas tank about to explode? Are there people or pets inside? The list of uncertainties, doubts, and dangers is endless, yet firefighters do it every day. Leading fearlessly is in their job description.

They are able to lead fearlessly because they are prepared physically and mentally to navigate the challenges of the task before them. Running into a burning building unprepared isn't living fearlessly; it's living foolishly. A strong leader knows the difference.

I had the privilege of coaching a group of firefighters on leadership, and when I shared my awe at their ability and willingness to run into a fire filled with unknown dangers, determined to deal with whatever challenges presented themselves, Chief Buxton responded by saying, "Brendan, you did the same as a turnaround CEO running into burning companies."

> They are able to lead fearlessly because they are prepared physically and mentally to navigate the challenges of the task before them.

"Not quite the same," I said.

"When you went through the front door, I'm pretty sure you didn't know all the problems the company had, but at the end of each day, you could see what was accomplished, and then you went home and got a good night's sleep because when the bell rang the next morning, you had to approach the new day with the same amount of strength, ability, and energy because lives were at stake," said the chief.

I laughed and said, "There are some similarities, but they end with 'lives were at stake.' I wasn't pulling anyone out of a burning building."

"That's true. We deal with life and death, but you deal with employment or unemployment—can someone pay their rent, buy their kid clothes? That takes the same strength, ability, and adrenaline that we draw on to fight fires."

The truth is we all have the opportunity to access our strength, ability, and resilience to live and lead fearlessly every day, even if we're not running into burning buildings. Keep building your skills, mental strength, and resilience every day. Embrace positive thoughts about your desired outcomes and commit to doing what it takes to seeing it through. This sounds inspiring, but I don't want to paint any illusion that fear won't exist. It will. Yet you can develop the ability to overcome it. If you prepare as best as you can, when the initial jolt of fear sets in and your mind moves to uncertainty and your body wants to curl up with doubt, you will be able to stand tall and recognize these feelings and emotions and then channel your strength in a different direction. You will be able to run toward the fear, not from it. Let me repeat—you will be able to run toward your fear and face it head-on. In doing so, you will truly be living fearlessly.

We can choose to be the light others look to, the hope others rely on, and the positive among the doomsayers. Honestly, doesn't the world really need us now more than ever? Are you ready to take on the responsibility of being fearless as something bigger than you and a way you can positively impact every person you come into touch with? Then let's get started!

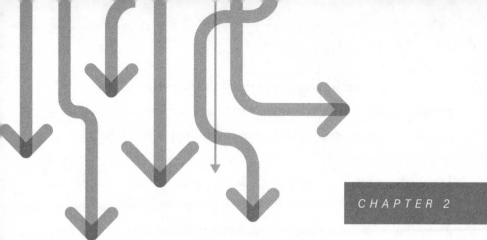

CHAPTER 2

Be a Leader

The moment I chose to be a leader was the first day of football practice in rural New Hampshire when I was in third grade. Coach Buchanan circled up all the eight-year-old players and asked for someone to get in the middle and lead jumping jacks. I'm not sure what possessed me, but something moved me to jump in the middle of the circle at Artillery Field and start counting. I was immediately smitten with leadership and have made a conscious decision to lead every day since.

Making the decision to be a leader is the *greatest gift* you could ever give yourself in life, and who doesn't like gifts? Leadership not only provides you the opportunity to own any fear, uncertainty, and doubt you may have but it also gives you the responsibility to remove fear, uncertainty, and doubt from others.

Leadership is inspiring, exhilarating, *and* challenging. Leadership is not management. Managing tasks is straightforward: see the task, do the task, done. Leading people is not so easy. As a leader, you must develop skills to set a vision people can follow, develop relationships so people will want to follow, and set goals so they know how to follow.

As a Fearless Leader, you will have fulfilling days, confusing days, and downright tough days, and the scary part can be that you don't know what each day will bring. But that's what makes true leaders special; they overcome the fear and make the *daily decision* to lead. Every day is an opportunity to unwrap a gift, accept the unknown challenge, and bask in the rewards. Your daily decision to accept the mantle of leadership makes the world a less fearful place.

Welcome to your leadership *journey*. It truly is a journey and not a one-stop *destination*. Becoming a strong and Fearless Leader is a lifelong pursuit, and each day serves as a new lesson and teaching moment, preparing us for greater opportunities in life. As you are presented these opportunities, and we both know they are really challenges in disguise, no matter how tough it is, think of the strength you are building and how much more prepared you will be for the next even bigger opportunity. That is one of the blessings of leadership; each challenge and opportunity makes us stronger for the next one if we embrace it, if we lean in, and if we commit to leading fearlessly.

Daily Decision

Throughout my life I've pursued every leadership opportunity I could because I truly believed Fearless Leadership was the gift God had bestowed on me. I must admit, though, there were days growing up I wished God had made me smarter, more athletic, or better looking. Why? Well, I had to work really hard to get good grades in school, I had to work out a little longer to be competitive on the athletic field, and I had to use my sense of humor to win girls over.

Leading, while I did work at it, didn't require that same level of effort. It came natural to me. Just as someone may be a whiz at math, while others are exceptional at sports, I found the path I was best at was leadership, and I made the decision every day to find a way to lead. I captained every team I was given the chance to, even when I wasn't the best on the team. I ran for class president all through high school and college, and I've been blessed to have the opportunity to lead companies as president and CEO six times across different industries from technology to finance to automotive.

Show up as a Leader Every Day

Within five minutes of meeting Kirsten Rhodes, I knew she was a natural leader, and I hired her on the spot. Kirsten oozed all the intangibles of a strong leader; I could feel her strong work ethic and positive energy as soon as we began conversing. Here's the funny part. I didn't hire her for a leadership position. When Kirsten first came on board in 1999, she was in an individual contributor role, but that didn't stop her from doing whatever needed to be done in a leadership way. Kirsten may not have been on the org chart, but if you observed her, you would've thought she was a vice president by the way she held herself, by the way she commanded influence, and by how she related to others and was able to inspire them to work successfully with her on projects. It wasn't long before Kirsten was promoted to a manager role and then a director role within the company.

Fast-forward to today, Kirsten Rhodes is the highly successful San Francisco managing principal at Deloitte LLP. I caught up with her in 2021 for the first time in years, and I was amazed at how she still exuded the same big, positive energy she had when I first met her. It was clear that she made the daily decision to be the best version of herself she could be and shared that energy and best version of herself with everyone around her. That is the magic that propels people in their career and in their personal life because people like Kirsten are the people we all want to be around. So what's her secret to showing up as a leader every day?

When I think about my personal leadership style and how it's evolved, I realize it encompasses two distinct foundations. The first is my family position and my role in it. The second is my naturally competitive spirit.

I'm the oldest of four girls, the second mama in the family, if you will. My role as the eldest gave me the unique opportunity to build leadership qualities and to perfect my ability to motivate others. Growing up, I was incredibly driven, both academically and athletically. I swam competitively up until high school. In high school and college, I played the piano and sang competitively, winning competitions throughout the state of Colorado. I was also a cheerleader and student council member, both of which taught me the importance of contributing to a team and giving back.

Shortly after I graduated from college, I accepted a job offer in California. I had never visited the state and didn't know a single person who lived there. Still, at 21, I hopped on a plane for San Jose to start the next chapter in my life. I lived in a hotel for the first week, bought a car by myself, and slept on a colleague's floor until I found an apartment.

My dad's reaction to this incredible risk? "Oh, I think you'll be home in six months." I don't know if he intended for his comments to motivate me or not, but it certainly had that effect. My immediate objective: to beat his prediction, and to prove him wrong. So, I stuck with it and thirty-one years later, I'm the Managing Principal of one of the largest US markets of a global company. Taking a risk, and proving my dad wrong, definitely paid off and helped me develop solutions to the situations that challenge any leader.

Over the years, I've built upon that foundation. I make sure that each and every day, I show up as an authentic and inspirational mentor, advisor, and manager. I've learned numerous invaluable lessons from incredibly successful leaders along my career journey who set a purpose and led with empathy to understand their team members' short-term or long-term challenges and goals. I've had leaders who are thoughtful and transparent communicators, who recognize the need to build trust amongst team members.

Some of my key mentors were incredible partners who ran exceptionally large, complex teams. What I loved about them is how far advanced they were in the definition of leadership. Rather than simply accepting their title as proof of leadership, they consistently worked on their leadership style. I also appreciated that they prioritized well-being, a critical element that we must all continue to bring to the forefront. Those experiences helped shape how I think of my role in mentoring the next generation of professionals. I think about how I can ensure I'm continuing to broaden the skill sets of the utility members on my team. Additionally, I commit to listening and ensure they feel comfortable enough to be transparent with their needs.

In the future, I plan to continue to be intentional about how I lead. I will continue to be transparent in my communication, inspire others, celebrate successes, and show gratitude for team members. I will expect a high level of accountability, via tangible measures, from the team and from each team member. Above all, I've realized that when leaders share their own goals and aspirations with others, they inspire the kind of trust and confidence that enables leaders and teams to achieve their vision ... whatever that vision may be.

Leadership Is a Journey, Not a Destination

I was heading to Europe! I know that in today's world, traveling abroad is no big deal, but at the time, it was a big deal to me. Not only was I traveling outside of the United States for the first time but I also had created a masterful plan to help my colleagues in the United Kingdom, Germany, and France deal with a growth issue, and I could barely contain my excitement—oh, man, were they going to be impressed.

The day of the meeting, I was at the hotel gym at 5:00 a.m., getting my sweat on and rehearsing my presentation one final time. Showered and dressed in my best suit, I met my boss John in the lobby so we could grab the Tube together.

"You ready, Brendan?" John asked.

"Oh, I'm ready. My plan is going to blow their socks off," I said, trying not to sprint to the station.

Our European colleagues welcomed us into their offices, and we exchanged the usual pleasantries. Finally, my moment arrived. Everyone was seated around the table. All eyes were on me, and I dived in. No gentle lead-up, no encouragement for dialogue, just a passionate presentation of my incredible plan. I finished with a huge smile and a "Pretty great, right? What do you think?"

That's when I realized I was the only one smiling, the only one impressed. My European colleagues were exchanging silent but knowing glances. John was staring at me; I think if he could have, he would have tossed me out of the room.

My plan went from amazing to blown up in seven words through two translators. "That's not how we do it here." I was stunned. We worked for the same company, and my plan would definitely lead to success, so why weren't they applauding? In that moment the three elements of fear began to set in and consume my being—fear of failure, uncertainty about what to do, and doubt that I had the skills to solve this new problem.

Luckily for me, John was further along his leadership journey than I was. He grabbed the reins, brought his Fearless Leadership to the situation, and helped me navigate the cultural and communication challenges. Once John took over, built a cultural bridge, and allowed them to agree we had a growth issue, we could then and only then talk about my plan on how to solve it. That's right; in my excitement, I had barged in, telling them how to solve their "problem" without providing them the opportunity to discuss and acknowledge that they had a problem, what they understood the problem to be, or any ideas that they might have to solve the problem.

John mentored me through that process, demonstrating the importance of listening to others and respecting that we are not all the same and that we do not all think alike or approach things in the same way. It was also a lesson in humility. If I had continued to focus only on my goals for the meeting and had been too stubborn to step back and read the room or allow John to take the reins, I absolutely would have failed. Thankfully, through John's mentorship, I only stumbled and then got up, dusted myself off, and grew as a leader. A sincere thanks to John for coaching me through my inaugural global trip.

No matter where you are on your leadership journey, please remember there is no final destination, there is no "arrival" location, and there is no mountaintop; there are simply more places to visit, more people to understand, more lessons to learn, and more problems to solve.

Even World Championships Aren't Final Destinations

What a loss it would have been for the Cleveland (Indians) Guardians if Terry Francona had decided that the Boston Red Sox's historic 2004 World Series win was his final leadership destination. What a well-deserved destination and incredible high on which to retire. After all, Francona didn't just lead them to a World Series victory in 2004 but he also led them through two historic firsts along the way. In the 2004 American League Championship Series, the Sox came back from a 0–3 deficit to beat their archrivals, the Yankees, and become the first MLB team to rally from three games down to a win and the first to force a seventh game from a 0–3 starting point.

That this history-making win was eighty-six years in the making and that it was a curse that Boston fans prayed for more than eight decades to be released from made it a crowning glory, a worthy final destination. But great leaders, Fearless Leaders, forge beyond the highs, beyond the crowning achievements, because for them leading others to greatness is a lifelong pursuit.

Francona went on to lead the Red Sox to five playoffs and a second World Series win before moving over to Cleveland's clubhouse and turning them from a 68–94 scorecard to 92–70 in his first year. Under his leadership Cleveland reached the postseason five-out-of-eight seasons, and in 2013 and 2016, Francona was named American League manager of the year.[9]

New England Patriots' Bill Belichick, love him or hate him, is another high-achieving coach who, no matter how great the win is—six Super Bowl titles, nine AFC championships, seventeen division titles—makes the daily decision to return and lead every single day to continue to commit to his leadership journey one game at a time.

Both of these coaches are best known for their incredible successes, but not every team they coached won world championships or broke records. Before joining the Red Sox, during Francona's four seasons (1997–2000) with the Phillies, the club never rose above third place in the National League East.[10] Belichick was fired from the Cleveland Browns after five seasons and a 36–44–0 record.[11] Despite the challenges, they kept showing up, willing to lead, to learn, to work hard, and to become the fearless and incredibly successful leaders they are today. Yes, they both have world champion titles, but it's not the titles that make them great leaders.

---

9   Jim Ingraham, "Terry Francona Poised to Make Cleveland Indians History," July 22, 2021, accessed March 29, 2022, https://www.forbes.com/sites/jimingraham/2021/07/22/terry-francona-poised-to-make-cleveland-indians-history/?sh=60c075bb13e8.

10   "Terry Francona," Baseball Reference, accessed March 29, 2022, https://www.baseball-reference.com/managers/francte01.shtml.

11   "Bill Belichick Coaching Record," accessed March 29, 2022, https://pro-football-history.com/coach/21/bill-belichick-bio.

This, of course, doesn't just apply to sports leaders but the same is true for Fearless Leaders across all industries as well. Let's look at Mary Barra, CEO and chair of General Motors, whose success, to me, is the epitome of a Fearless Leadership journey, starting on the assembly line at GM at the age of eighteen, working hard every day, owning her job as if it were the only one she would ever have, and not only seizing every available opportunity but also creating opportunity through her commitment, diligence, and willingness to listen and learn.

One thing that distinguishes those who really make a difference in life, those who really contribute, is passion and hard work. Remember: hard work beats talent if talent doesn't work hard. So don't be content to work around the edges of your profession. Don't wait to be invited to important meetings or asked to work on crucial assignments. Instead, do what it takes to ensure that you're in the middle of your business. Speak up. Volunteer. Show your enthusiasm. Knock on doors. As an employee your enthusiasm will make your job more interesting and get you noticed. And as a manager, your passion will inspire others to join your team and work as hard as you to accomplish great things.

—MARY BARRA, 2014 UNIVERSITY OF MICHIGAN
COMMENCEMENT SPEECH

Named one of the 100 Most Influential People in the World by *Time* magazine in 2014 and one of the World's 50 Great Leaders by *Fortune* magazine in 2018, Barra, like Francona and Belichick, boasts some pretty impressive achievements, yet Barra shows no indication that she has reached a "final leadership destination." In fact, with her commitment to zero crashes, zero emissions, and zero congestion, it seems like she's just getting started. Barra's Fearless Leadership is transforming not only General Motors and the auto industry but also how the world moves in a way that makes everyone's life better. Barra is a leader people will always follow.

The Title Doesn't Make the Leader

A shiny brass CEO nameplate on the office door doesn't make you a Fearless Leader. It might make you a formal leader, one who tells people what to do and checks the boxes on a management to-do list, but that's not Fearless Leadership. I've had my fair share of experience with leaders, some who had *the* title and some who didn't. I'd like to share a couple with you.

CEO Charlie had an impressive résumé. He was educated. He was accomplished. He was someone you wanted on your team—until he wasn't. To be fair I met CEO Charlie in his later leadership years. It may be that, at some point along his journey, he was everything his résumé purported him to be, but my experience with him made me wonder, "How the heck did this guy get where he is?"

Charlie came into the office a couple of days a week, spent his other workdays on the golf course, and in my view seemed disengaged with his leadership team and the company as a whole. Over several months I could see that his ability to impact the business was withering. His people stopped following him because he wasn't leading them anywhere. Eventually, in order to get them to follow, he'd wave his title around.

> It's not the title; it's how you show up.

For a Fearless Leader and their followers, the title is not the motivating factor. People listen to a Fearless Leader because they want to hear what they have to say. People follow a Fearless Leader because they believe in them. It should never be because CEO Charlie says, "Listen up, everyone. I'm the CEO, and this is what I need you to do." Remember when Kirsten joined as an individual contributor, yet everyone viewed her as a vice president? It's not the title; it's how you show up.

When you believe you've arrived, that you've reached your final leadership destination, and that you no longer need to maintain the energy level, the passion, and the stamina that got you to where you are, you don't just sit in the status quo but you also fall behind. Why? Because the world, people, business, and technology continue to evolve around you. You may retain your title for a while, but I guarantee someone else has taken the reins.

Now meet Tye Kuhlman. I first learned about Tye in my leadership meetings in my role as turnaround CEO. Tye wasn't in the meetings. In fact, he didn't have a leadership title or role, but what he did have was positive influence. I can't count the number of times his name came up in our leadership meetings. It seemed no matter what was being discussed, at some point, an executive would say, "Let me check with Tye."

It didn't take me long to be introduced to Tye, to recognize his leadership potential, and to invite him to be a member of the leadership team. Not everyone on the team was comfortable with adding an account manager to the table, one who didn't directly report to me, but regardless of Tye's title or who his direct supervisor was, one thing was clear: Tye was highly important to the organization. People sought him out, he was knowledgeable, and he was willing to share that knowledge.

That singular move of acknowledging and respecting what Tye was already bringing to the table and faith in his potential to soar transformed him from a confident and capable individual to a confident and successful executive leader. Within the company Tye went from account manager to director to vice president. The titles didn't make him a leader—he was already leading—but moving into an executive position provided him the opportunity to motivate, inspire, and lead even more people to make great things happen. Leadership is the gift that keeps on giving, and I encourage you to pass it on.

Greatest Gift

Imagine having the opportunity every day to assist a teammate for the game-winning goal and to celebrate victory as a team. Accepting the gift of leadership gives you that opportunity every day. And your team stretches across all aspects of your life—your family, friends, colleagues, and community members. Your assist is like a spark of electricity sending positive vibes and waves across teammates. Leadership gives you the ability to positively impact the lives of many. As solitary individuals we impact a limited number of people, but as we make the daily decision to be a leader, and we do that over a lifetime, the impact becomes exponential.

In the midst of COVID-19, I had many opportunities to see my team step up and succeed in the most trying of times, but one particular experience really blew me away. At Merchants Fleet we have two businesses, a business-to-business company and a business-to-consumer company. One operates commercial fleets, and the other sells preowned cars. So you can imagine these are dramatically different businesses requiring distinctly different skill sets and experience.

Our consumer auto business developed a COVID-19 case, and as an incredibly employee-first company, we shut our preowned showroom down and closed the business for the foreseeable future until we could get everyone tested and returned to work safely. Halfway through the first day of being closed and unable to serve our great clients, a group of leaders in our commercial fleet business took the lead.

These individuals, with absolutely no experience selling preowned cars to consumers, put their day jobs on hold and reopened the dealership to welcome our clients back into the showroom and to get them behind the wheel of the cars they needed. On the surface this sounds pretty cool but maybe not amazing until you stop and think about a few things:

1. No one had any training in how to sell cars.
2. No one knew how to do all that crazy paperwork that is required when someone buys a car.
3. No one had the time to put their day job on hold to take on a new job they didn't know how to do.
4. No one had anything to gain personally by doing this. Their paid day jobs were Monday through Friday, yet they all came in on their days off on Saturday and Sunday for no pay to help out their team members and the company.

And that is where I had the chance to witness leadership in action and watch one group of people provide another group that was unable to work due to COVID-19 restrictions the greatest gift possible.

The senior leader, Adam Secore, held an early morning training session on how to sell a car. For context the students were all leaders in the operations of the other business. They were individuals who were more familiar with driving operational efficiency and productivity than they were with car pricing, test-drives, and warranties. But they all strapped in and took notes on how to sell a car, do the paperwork, and please the consumers.

An hour later the dealership opened on schedule. Prospective clients came through the doors, and introverted operational specialists became extroverted sales professionals! So how was that even possible? How did people with twenty-plus years of experience in one area pivot over a breakfast training session and a few motivational words to a completely different role? *Leadership.*

When we embrace our gift of leadership, we can do the extraordinary. I am hopeful that you will seize this opportunity to give yourself the gift of leadership. And if you are already leading, I hope you continue to share your gift with others every day.

Never Too Young to Lead

I chose to be a leader the first day of football practice when I was just eight years old, and I can honestly say that it was one of the best decisions I've ever made. No one is too young to make that choice or too young to be offered the opportunity to develop their leadership skills. That belief is what led me to an opportunity to run kid leadership academies with the Police Athletic League (PAL) in Nashua, New Hampshire. At what we called Victory Academies, the PAL staff and I would teach basic leadership skills to a group of kids who were in the third to eighth grade. These kids were coming to PAL for a variety of after-school and athletic programs.

What I always found fascinating in these sessions was the inability of some kids to see themselves as leaders; they'd decided at an early age that they didn't fit that bill. We'd be walking them through strength, courage, faith, and other core characteristics of being a good leader, and some of the kids would say, "Yeah, I don't see myself as a leader."

I'd ask them, "Why don't you see yourself as a leader?" What it came down to was their narrow view of a leader and not being able to see themselves in that role. For kids, their idea of a leader is often the superstar of sports, movies, or music, and if they don't see themselves as the star football or basketball player or lead singer, they assume they're not leadership material. In some cases they simply haven't been exposed to who they think of as leaders in their personal life, and they again make an assumption. This time that assumption is that their path forward can only be the same path as those in their immediate circle.

I always challenge their beliefs, and for a kid who played sports, I'd say, "You can be captain of your sports team."

"But I'm not the best player on my team," would be a standard reply. I'd go on to explain that they didn't have to be the best player to be a leader and helped them see what their leadership skills are. That would go something like this.

"Do people like you?"

"Yeah."

"OK. Do you know what that means?"

"No."

"That means that you can be influential."

"Huh?"

"Being influential means that people want to follow you. Do you know what happens when people want to follow you?"

"I'm their leader?"

"Yes! You become their leader. Whether you have the *C* on your shirt as captain or not, if people are following you, you're leading. You can use your great personality to attract others."

By simply giving a kid a glimpse of themselves as a leader, I could see the start of their transformation. They'd sit up taller, and instead of staring at the piece of paper with the question "What are your positive attributes?" they'd start writing down as fast as they could all that is good about them and seeing those qualities as leadership strengths. Programs like PAL are often the spark that these kids need to visualize their aspirations and believe they can achieve them. I'll let

Shaun Nelson, the executive director of Nashua PAL, share how they ignite the leadership spark in their kids.

At PAL we believe it's important to help kids develop the right leadership skills because we believe strongly that kids, especially kids in tough neighborhoods, are going to be leaders of their neighborhoods whether they have guidance or not, and if they don't have the opportunity to develop positive leadership skills, they'll become the wrong kind of leader. Everything we do at PAL's after-school program is broken into three categories: education, activity, and leadership.

Leadership is a big one, and although kids never come in asking for structure or asking for leadership skills, they thrive in it. The young people who come to our center every day will start their afternoon doing homework and then have a snack. After that it can be anything from a community service project that they are leading or a simple, fun activity. The key is that, through everything the kids experience at PAL, we expose them to the right types of leaders. Those leaders include staff and volunteers working in the program and leaders in the community whom, through various programs, we connect the kids with. Providing that exposure to positive leadership role models helps provide the kids with inspiration to feed the fire that we have hopefully ignited.

Fearless Leadership is possible for everyone, and if we can help fan the flames of leadership in kids until they are at the point of being able to motivate themselves in that direction, they will be successful, and in that success, they will help build other leaders.

We find that making space for creative conversations in small groups or individually really helps kids discover their ambitions. We ask questions like, "What do you see yourself doing when you grow up?" Whatever that profession or goal is, we walk them through the path they would need to take to make that happen. When we ask, "Who's a good leader in your community?" they may say their teacher or a grandmother down the street who helps them occasionally. Sometimes it's a sports star. No matter who they see as a leader, we'll talk about what the attributes of those leaders are by asking questions like, "Why did you choose that person?" Often the responses are about consistency and motivation. Once those attributes are defined, we talk with the kids about how they can get from where they are, regardless of circumstances, to where they want to be.

It's amazing to watch the transformation in real time. Here's just one example. One summer evening while we had a basketball clinic going on, we saw a young girl pushing her younger sister in a stroller. It was late for these two kids to be out on their own. We started a conversation and learned more about what was going on in their lives, and eventually, the older girl, who was twelve, became a member. We kept having creative conversations wrapped up in field trips and what I call glitter and glue—arts and crafts activities are like a magical magnet for kids. All these actions combined kept her moving on the right path, and now she's thriving.

This now seventeen-year-old is playing volleyball for her high school team, and her sister is now a PAL member. They still have plenty of challenges, but now she's got a solid direction and understands some of the limitations that are going on in her life. Those limitations no longer define her because she's able to identify them and learn how to move on in spite of them.

When you see kids like this begin to become confident advocates for themselves and their peers, when they can voice that to us, that's when the leadership begins to shine through.

Conversations with Kids That Lead to Real Change

Shaun and his team recently had guided conversations with a group of six kids in the program. It started with a glitter-and-glue activity during which the staff helped guide the oldest kid (aged ten) to rally the efforts of the group. They talked about neighborhoods. Was there an area that they liked or disliked about their own neighborhood? What did they think was beautiful about their neighborhood? Through those conversations, over time this small group led by one ten-year-old decided that they wanted to enhance one of the parks near the PAL center.

They started spending time cleaning up the park. We gave them a little money, and they fixed up a park bench. Then the magic really began to happen as they talked about community leaders who could help with their effort. One ten-year-old believed the park where she and her friends spent a lot of time needed some love, and she led an effort that triggered a conversation at city hall, which triggered a conversation with the utility company, which resulted in lights being put up in this park, an older stage area being revamped for future concerts, a beautiful mural painted, and significant infrastructure improvements. It's amazing to be able to stand back and say to a kid, "Because of your leadership, your neighborhood has a beautiful, safe park."

The gift of leadership is possible for everyone at any age. Are you intentionally sharing your gift of leadership?

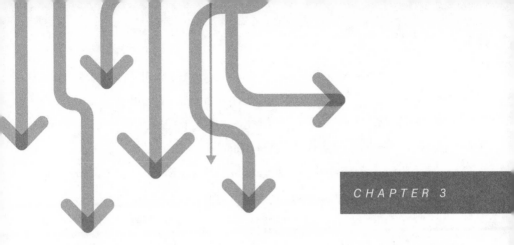

CHAPTER 3

Be Good

Being good is all about our core *values* as a person. Every one of us has a set of core values that has been built from a young age into adulthood. From day one the people who have raised us—our parents, relatives, guardians, and friends—have been imprinting values upon us. When you were young and impressionable, you were just young and impressionable. Remember words like these:

"Show respect for your sister."

"That type of behavior may be OK for your friends but not you."

"Do your chores. Everybody fulfills their role in this family."

Those words instilled the values of respect, strength, and hard work.

Take a minute and reflect on words you remember from your childhood. Now let's fast-forward from your childhood to adulthood. How many of those early values do you still hold close, what new ones have you developed along the way, and how do you live those values and instill them in those you lead? The six key values I choose to live by are *strength, courage, faith, service, humility,* and *leadership.*

61

Being a Fearless Leader requires many traits like intellect, compassion, and perseverance. But if you dig down and look at what's really serving as a foundation for everything else, it's *strength* in all its aspects—physical, mental, emotional, and spiritual.

Without strength a leader cannot act with courage. *Courage* is a value that is acquired over time: the courage to lean into your fears and confront them, the courage to believe in a positive outcome amid uncertainty, and the courage to channel your mind, body, and soul to overcome your doubts.

Fearless Leaders have *faith* in themselves and in others and instill faith in those around them. Fearless Leaders have the faith to succeed. They believe in positive outcomes, even when the facts and data suggest otherwise.

Fearless Leaders are willing and enthusiastic servants. They understand the sacrifice of *service* and the rewards for being the person who makes it happen in the background. The intrinsic internal and eternal flame of serving a greater good burns bright inside every Fearless Leader.

Humility is a value that shapes our legacy. As a Fearless Leader, you will have the courage to seize opportunities and overcome challenges, and your faith will lead you to exhilarating victories. Fearless Leaders keep an equilibrium between their successes and their servitude. Fearless Leaders serve for the purpose of their vision in life to accomplish something bigger than themselves and do so to benefit the greater good.

Leadership is a value that stands the test of time and is a summation of your life's work. The Fearless Leader accepts the responsibility of the goal, builds a team with the skills and experience to achieve the goal, and lights the path toward the goal on a daily basis.

Strength

Sometimes in life we meet a person who exemplifies the values we hold most dear; a person who shows up every day ready to lead and serve others with compassion, courage, and humility; or a person who lifts others up even when they are facing tremendous personal challenges. Jeanine Charlton is one of those people, and while her courage, humility, leadership, and service to others are exemplary, her true superpower is her incredible strength.

Jeanine first stumbled into her career in technology when, on the encouragement of a friend, she walked into the recruiting office of EDS and was hired on the spot. Starting out in human resources, Jeanine immediately took advantage of EDS's extensive and supportive training environment. As Jeanine tells it,

> EDS was a company with a strong culture of helping people grow and develop. For those of us who were willing to work hard and who wanted to advance, we were given incredible opportunities to learn new skills, and so I learned technical skills through on-the-job training and experiences. Additionally, I was blessed early with leaders who really took an interest in me and mentored me, providing me the confidence that I needed to take on more responsibility.

> It wasn't long before I set a leadership goal for myself: to achieve the level of account manager before I was thirty. Account manager was a big deal in our environment because that's when you were given the responsibilities to manage a client relationship, a delivery team, and a P&L. I worked hard and was promoted to account

manager when I was twenty-eight! I had a wonderful mentor who became a sponsor for me and provided me that first management opportunity, and that's when I felt my career begin to really accelerate.

Jeanine continued to work hard, to learn, and to seek out opportunities for growth, establishing her credentials as a top technical leader. Her Fearless Leadership paid off, and midcareer she was asked to lead the company's biggest client, the Navy-Marine Corps Intranet (NMCI).

By saying yes, I was agreeing to oversee the company's biggest client with a $1.5 billion budget, and I was also stepping into a role in the public sector, something I had never done before. Not only is business done a bit differently between public and commercial business but the politics are also navigated differently—there was a lot I had to learn quickly. What wasn't new for me, but still challenging, was working in a male-dominated environment. All of that combined, I felt that I would have to outwork and outsmart everybody else to be successful.

The promotion came at a difficult time in Jeanine's personal life, and the required relocation with two teenagers would be challenging, but Jeanine saw it as an opportunity for a fresh start, and she and her children made the move from Michigan to Virginia. Before she could begin her new position with NMCI, both of Jeanine's children developed serious health issues. Starting a new job in a new state with two sick children and no support system was make-or-break time for her.

My company had great expectations for me overseeing their biggest account, so I didn't share my personal challenges with them. The last thing I wanted to do was sow doubt in their minds that with everything going on in my personal life, I wouldn't be able to manage my new work responsibilities.

I remember walking into the office my first day and telling myself, "You got this because failure is not an option." My kids gave me my strength because, at the end of the day, they needed me to make our life work.

Jeanine not only made her kids' lives work—they are now healthy, thriving adults—but she also was highly successful at NMCI and has gone on to many other successes in the field of leadership and technology as indicated by her appointment to the National Diversity Council Top 50 Most Powerful Women in Tech in 2020, winning the 2020 Chicago CIO of the Year ORBIE Award, winning the 2021 CIO 100, and being a finalist of the 2022 National CIO of the Year ORBIE Award. Jeanine's success has been built on her work ethic, her courage to seek out and seize opportunities, and her sheer strength to keep moving forward even in the most difficult of circumstances.

4 Types of Strength Every Leader Should Possess

Strength takes on many forms: physical, mental, emotional, and spiritual. Fearless Leaders strike a balance and develop all aspects of strength. Stay healthy physically, stay sharp mentally, stay balanced emotionally, and stay centered spiritually. Building strength should be a daily habit because fear, uncertainty, and doubt strike on their own schedule, not ours. And we must build reserves of strength to fight fear when it strikes unexpectedly. Here are my thoughts on how to build and reinforce across each aspect of strength.

Physical Strength

Most great leaders are willing to put in plenty of hours to help others and bring the best ideas to the table. To do that you can't skimp on taking care of your body. Enjoying nutritious food, staying hydrated, hitting the gym, and getting enough shut-eye all work together. Tackling those four key pillars of physical self-care—food, water, exercise, and sleep—can protect you from getting sick and give you the energy you need to reach the finish line.

Mental Strength

People are capable of incredible things. They just need to believe in themselves enough to go after what they want. In this regard that old saying of "Mind over matter" really does ring true. It's mental toughness that lets you pivot and solve problems on the fly no matter what other people might pressure you to do.

Ask yourself what sources and outlets you can utilize to grow mentally. Just about anything that helps you feel recharged is valid, but self-care activities like spending time with loved ones who can engage in compassionate debates, wandering outside where it's green, or reading a good book are popular choices that can reinvigorate your positive energy.

Emotional Strength

As much as businesses must lean on analytics, emotions are part of the pie too. You're going to be confused or unsure sometimes. You're going to feel pride and excitement. And yes, pumping up your team is part of the job. People will look to see how you react in certain situations. The more you keep your cool, show real empathy, and get excited about the right things, the more they will too.

To cultivate amazing emotional strength, don't be shy about communicating what you consider to be toxic. Draw clear boundaries. As so many experts point out, sometimes you might not have a choice about your circumstances, but you always have a choice about how you react. Learn to recognize what triggers you. Practice taking time to cool off. Think things through, even as you acknowledge the reality of what you and others feel.

Above all invest in good people. Reconnecting regularly with others who can support you will give you incredible balance that makes it easier to face everything else. You never have to do anything alone.

Spiritual Strength

Spiritual strength simply means connecting to a deeper place and purpose in the universe, whether that's following a faith or understanding how the energy of everything is linked. When you believe in this type of higher power, it's easy to feel more grounded with plenty of reserves to draw on.

What builds your spiritual strength will depend a lot on your core philosophies and values. Prayer or faith-based services, practicing mindfulness, reading inspiring stories, and even volunteering and seeing your influence on others are good ways to nourish your soul.

> You can't correct weaknesses you don't see.

Even though you can foster individual types of strengths to become a more Fearless Leader, see the big picture. Understand that the stronger you get in one area, the stronger you'll likely become in the others. Don't underestimate the positive influence your personal strength will have on your company culture, as it spreads through your team. Let people see your journey. The more others see you conquer, the more they'll be inspired and trust you to handle bigger opportunities.

Remember, you can't correct weaknesses you don't see. Put your ego aside. Ask for feedback. Stay objective and have faith that you can learn from your experiences and mistakes. With this work-in-progress, self-forgiving attitude, you'll stay motivated to get through every stage of your life and have the strength to do it.

Courage

I have always been puzzled by the reason why some people got the corner office and some didn't and why promotions sometimes went to the most qualified person and sometimes didn't. Over the past decade, I became a management scientist of sorts, looking into this issue. There were a few obvious findings and a few big surprises. The obvious things had to do with relationships, influence, and emotional intelligence. The big surprise was that many people whose career fell short or who didn't receive the proper recognition lacked one mighty trait: *courage*.

So what does courage really mean in the context of your career? *Courage* is the ability to seize opportunity and take bold action in the face of fear, uncertainty, doubt, difficulty, and/or danger. I discovered that it wasn't being overlooked that kept most people from taking the next step in their career; they simply didn't seize their moment. I witnessed instances where individuals had brilliant solutions to complex challenges but failed to take the bold action and present their idea. They were overwhelmed by fear of failure, uncertainty about the outcome, and general self-doubt.

Just like the lion in *The Wizard of Oz*, we may not all have courage right now, but it does not mean we cannot develop it. Courage is simply the decision to take a bold action, even though it may be frightening. To truly live and lead fearlessly, you must be willing to step out on a limb from time to time to take a challenge, face doubt, and have the *courage to fail*.

Going Further Faster

"Listen up, team. You all did a great job over the past four months making the three-hundred-unit account with our delivery service client happen. I know it was tough, and it stretched us in new ways, but we did it, and we did it well. Now the client is launching a new initiative, and they've asked us to supply them with three thousand vehicles over the next ninety days and deploy them all over the country. I'm a yes. I know we'll figure out how to ramp up times ten. Everyone else in?"

If I had told you in chapter 1 that six months after John resisted my two new business start-ups even with permission for one to fail, he would be the one leading the charge to go from a three-hundred- to three-thousand-fleet commitment in ninety days with *zero* plan in place to make it happen, you wouldn't have believed me. But that's exactly what happened. Here's John's story.

I had been with the company for twenty-seven years when Brendan joined as CEO. In those almost three decades, never was I exposed to the concept of investing in future business. The culture had always been a transactional one. I own it for X. I sold it for Y; therefore, I made Z. Long-term strategy was never part of the con-versation; it was always sell and backfill, sell and backfill. I grew up in that culture, and having Brendan come in and tell me to order five hundred vehicles to start a new business before a plan was in place was completely foreign to me. Never had the company taken risks like that before, nor was anyone encouraged to take risks.

I remember having the discussion with the team and Brendan throwing out five hundred vehicles and me countering with fifty, worried that even that was too risky. Here I was the leader of the team, nervous and unwilling to take a risk, while all the people I supervised were sitting around the table, saying, "Let's do this. We got this." They're willingness made sense to me because they had been with the company for a shorter period, and they hadn't experienced the cultural history of avoiding failure at all costs. But it really made me sit back and think, "How fixed am I that the people I lead are sitting here, looking at me, saying, 'Come on, man. Let's go,' and I'm too nervous to say yes?" That was an eye-opening moment for me. It was my team's fearless perspective that gave me the courage to take that initial leap of faith. Once I crossed that threshold, though, I built momentum quickly.

One of my strengths is tactical execution, so once the decision was made, my instincts to think innovatively, to find solutions, and to move forward kicked in. Now I'm a 100 percent believer that getting out in front with a yes, with a vision, and then building the infrastructure for your future success enables an organization to go faster and further. It's also a far more rewarding strategy.

"Let's go for it. If we're not successful, we'll iterate. We'll try it again." That's the mantra I lead with every day.

Have the Courage to Fail and the Faith to Succeed

That is a phrase that has led me throughout my career. When people ask me where I came up with this saying, I can honestly reply that I have absolutely no idea. Sometimes I wish I had some grand, elaborate story of magic and mysticism, but even my oldest friends still tell me that I have always worn the phrase like a sash across my chest. Remarkably, I am thankful for this because I see that, instead of being based on a story, it is based on *being*. These words continue to guide me in all of my projects.

At first glance it may seem counterintuitive that you could have courage without faith or vice versa. However, there are those who do courageous things and say, "I'm going to train for the marathon, but there's no way I'll make it all twenty-six miles." Alternatively, some may have all the faith in the world that they have the ability to start their own business or write a book or coach a team, but they do not have the courage to make the bold move. Let's consider an example of this formula in action.

Gina is a high performer and a natural leader with a big appetite for career success. She has a career plan and has shared it with her boss. She is actively looking to propel her career forward within her current company and is willing to do whatever it takes. Because of this strong foundation, her boss comes to her one day and informs her that the company is creating a new division, and she has been selected to be on this exclusive team as a director. It is quite a bit above her current level and will place her among some great mentors, but her boss believes that this is the opportunity she has been seeking. However, she will have to relocate from her hometown in Rhode Island to California.

Gina has been presented with a career game changer and a life-changing decision. At this point we know that she is a high performer and has been effectively leading a small team. However, in order to make a bold career move that could propel her forward, she will have to muster the courage to say "yes" and the faith that everything will work out in her favor. So many factors come into play at this point. What will her husband say? Will she be able to do the job well? Will she like California? How will she find new friends? If she does not have the faith in herself or decides to turn the offer down, she may find herself stuck in the same position for a long time. This is, of course, OK if she is content with her current life, but Gina is the breadwinner and is very focused on career progression. Opportunities like this don't always come around. At this point Gina has two options:

Option 1: Gina and her husband are unsure of who the other team members are and what life in San Diego is like, so they decide that her current job is safe and secure. Gina decides to turn down the job offer.

Option 2: Gina and her husband seize the moment, believe in their future, and trust that something good will come of it. Gina accepts the promotion.

The path to success is dangerously littered, bumpy, and slippery with twists, turns, potholes, and hazards. But the path to success is also thrilling with opportunities to push you out of your comfort zone, see new geographies, meet new people, and learn new skills. Because each person's end goal is different, there is no real road map to success. However, there are certain steps that I have personally experienced and witnessed in many other executives. Based on my own stories and the stories of others, I have mapped out a nine-point success plan:

> The person you decide to spend the most time with will be the greatest contributing factor of your success.

1. **Partner.** The person you decide to spend the most time with will be the greatest contributing factor of your success. The right partner will inspire you and propel you forward. The wrong one will hold you back and distract you. In my career I have witnessed so many people give up tremendous opportunities because of partners who did not support them. Personally, when I was asked to relocate across the country two months before my wedding, it could have been the end of my not-yet-existent marriage. Lucky for me, my wife said yes. Lucky for me, we are still happily married after twenty-five years and twelve moves, zigzagging across the country.

2. **Plan.** Those who plan to succeed usually do. The plan does not have to be right or executed flawlessly, but it must exist. It is best to develop it annually and revisit it quarterly. A plan helps because it can define the purpose and end goal of one's career path. Since 1990 I have had a plan written out for my career. With every opportunity I have been presented with, I have referred back to this plan to make decisions. Whenever I ask highly motivated and successful executives what made them a success, proper planning is on everyone's list. Remember, your plan doesn't have to be right, and it can be changed, but you can only get to where you want to go if you define where you want to go.

3. **Focus.** A successful career requires a focused mindset. Sure, there are times for play and entertainment, but when it comes to game time, focus is paramount. We must focus our efforts, energy, time, and resources toward our career goals. As previously mentioned a plan can help put intent behind the focus. Time, effort, and energy cannot be recaptured, so harness their power in your selected craft.

4. **Commitment.** Following closely behind focus rests commitment. If you want to be successful, you must commit to yourself and your chosen career. If you want anyone to help you or commit to you, you first must commit to yourself. Eighty percent of people want to be successful, but less than 20 percent will be successful over a long period. The commitment to success, even through short-term challenges, is what makes the 60 percent difference.

5. **Sacrifice.** All decisions require trade-offs and sacrifices; career opportunities are no different. As a young leader, you have to say no to playtime frequently and put your head down to work on that extra presentation for the boss. I can tell you wholeheartedly that some late nights and weekends putting that special presentation or spreadsheet together helped me personally in many instances.

6. **Passion.** An important aspect to any successful career is figuring out what you are passionate about. What keeps you up at night? What excites you? I found that I had a passion for systems, models, and numbers, and thus, they became part of successful turnarounds I have done. I was able to exhibit a passion that was genuine, and others followed that passion. The pathway to success is unrelenting and tiring, and only people with true passion become truly successful.

7. **Energy.** Successful people know how to create and harness energy. There will be times you take on projects that you have zero passion for, but you must have the energy to sustain your progress. At this point in my career, I know that I need my morning workout to have the energy to perform throughout the day. With more energy, you can engage in more things

you are passionate about. Find out what fuels your energy and be consistent with fueling up.

8. **Leadership.** You find leadership in the success formula, and you find it here in the plan. Wonder if it's important? Leadership, by nature, creates opportunities. Opportunities create game-changing moments in your career. And these opportunities do not go to followers. To be a leader, be accountable, authentic, and consistent; work toward a common goal with your teams; and be willing to listen and take action.

9. **Courage and Faith.** If you have followed all the points up to now in your own career, then there will undoubtedly come a time when you are presented with a choice. Option 1 will be a very comfortable job in a comfortable place with comfortable benefits. Option 2 is unknown. It's scary and daunting and seemingly beyond your current experience. But option 2 is a game changer. It's the stepping-stone toward one heck of a career, and if you have made it to this point, then you have undeniably earned the right to say yes.

Gina passed on the career game changer, and hopefully, in the long run, that was the right decision for her and her family because an opportunity like this didn't come around again. The job was instead filled by a person named Jack who did an incredible job in the position, received tremendous recognition, and went on to have a successful, high-level career. Jack seized the moment, and his career took off.

Do you have the *courage* to take a bold action in the face of potential failure and the *faith* in yourself that if you seize the moment, success is possible?

Faith

Early in my career when I was living in Dallas and working for EDS, I got a call at home requesting my presence at a meeting that morning with my boss's boss. The moment I said, "Be right in," thoughts of doubt and uncertainty began racing through my mind. What had I done? Or maybe it was what I hadn't done. Either way this couldn't be good. Fortunately, I lived close to the office, so before too much fear, uncertainty, or doubt could cloud my thinking, I was sitting in the big boss's office.

"Good to see you, Brendan. How's everything going?" the big boss asked.

"Great, sir."

"Good, good. You know your name keeps coming up around here."

I felt a bead of sweat begin to form at my left temple. "It does, sir?"

"Yes, all positive, I assure you."

I cleared my throat. "Thank you, sir."

"As you know, we are making some changes around here, and one of those changes is appointing a new head of sales. I think you're the person to fill that role."

I tried not to fidget in my chair. "Excuse me, sir?"

"Brendan, I'm offering you the position of chief sales officer."

I was stunned. "Sir?"

"Yes?"

"I truly appreciate the offer, but I think there are others more qualified, others with more experience. Can I have some time to think it over?"

"Brendan, do you really think that I don't know that there are a lot of people with more years of experience than you?"

"No, of course not."

"What they don't have is my faith in their ability to get the job done. People believe in you; you have the power to instill confidence in others. You are the right person. I have faith in you. Now go get some work done and make me look good for this decision."

That day forever changed my career and subsequently my life. I seized my moment. The faith he instilled in me changed me as a leader. Every day of my life, I always had people who believed in me or who had faith in me, but this was different. This wasn't someone close to me, a family member, or a friend. This was a big-time corporate executive who placed his faith in me and asked me, in turn, to have faith in myself. As I left his office, I was on cloud nine with my feet barely on the ground and my mind a bit numb. If he has faith in me, I have more faith in me.

When somebody has more faith in themselves, they have more confidence, and that confidence does not stop when they walk out the door on Friday at five. That confidence stays with them when they run their 5K, when they join the school's PTA board, when they coach their kid's Little League team, or when they sing in their church's choir. Like the gift of leadership, faith is a gift that continues to grow within our beings.

Faith may take different forms for people—it may be spiritual and religious, and it may also be sheer confidence and belief. Faith requires Fearless Leaders to channel their powers when adversity strikes, when fear sets in, when uncertainty and doubt enter the room, and when others begin to weaken.

You Gotta Have Faith

When I met Chad Gundersen, producer of *The Chosen* series, twenty years ago, it was clear to me that this was a man committed to a purpose and had the faith to see it through. Just as I truly believe Fearless Leadership was the gift God had bestowed on me, Chad believes film production was the gift God had bestowed on him. In those early days, when I asked him why he was working as a personal trainer if his goal was to be a film producer, he said, "Well, I have to pay the bills, and personal training gives me the flexibility to work on my film producing." He was doing what he had to do to be what he was meant to be. I've watched Chad with admiration over the years pursue his purpose with passion and sacrifice, even when it meant his family would have to live through periods of instability and uncertainty, not knowing when his next job would come or if it would pay off.

> My wife, Amanda, has always had faith in me, but early on there were definitely moments when she questioned why I was doing what I was doing and why I wasn't going out and getting a real job. Then about twelve years ago, after our second child was born, we took a big step in our faith as a family. I was at a point where I was excelling in film producing, and we acknowledged that it was time for me to commit full-time. It was around that time that Amanda also came to the realization that this needed to be an us thing, that we needed to rally around my film producing as a family. Taking that leap of faith as a family definitely impacted the trajectory of my career and our lives. It all just keeps getting better and better.

Film producing—really anything in the entertainment business—can be brutal. You're only as good as your last movie, and your success can end in a flash. Fast-forward to today, Chad has had tremendous success in the movie industry while staying true to his convictions. Chad has embraced the four aspects of faith throughout his career: faith in himself (you have to believe in you), faith in a higher power (believe in something bigger than yourself, whatever that may mean for you), faith in others (surround yourself with people you believe in *and* let them know you have faith in them to be their best), and faith of others in him (embrace the faith that others have in you and pass it on).

My faith in God's plan for me, my faith in myself, and my family's faith in me is something I pass onto the people I surround myself with. As the producer, I take full responsibility for everything on the show. I say everything's my fault. I don't blame others. I don't yell. I'm one of those people who say, "Let's just solve the problem, and we'll talk about why it happened later." I made that choice as the overseer, and I believe my approach creates a lot of faith in others. They have faith in me because they know I support them. Our production company is a four-person team who fully supports each other. We have faith in each other that we always have each other's best interests at heart, that it's not all about me and it's not all about them. I think to have faith in others is about what you would do. What would you sacrifice for them and know that they would sacrifice that same thing for you? That is a big part of successfully moving forward together.

While Chad has had many filmmaking successes, *The Chosen* has been the crescendo of all the sacrifice, hard work, and years of faith that says that this was the path God chose for him.

> *The Chosen* is the largest crowdfunded show in history. It's been viewed almost half a billion times from all around the world, and we are about to enter our third season. It's just turned into this massive thing, and Amanda and I tell our kids, "You were a part of the sacrifice. You contributed to the impact we are making. You are part of this success that we are all living."

Service

Serve others relentlessly. Fearless Leaders are willing and enthusiastic servants. They understand the sacrifice of service and the rewards for being the person who makes it happen in the background. Serving silently at times is challenging because we all want to be recognized on some level. But it is the intrinsic internal and eternal flame of serving a greater good that burns bright inside every Fearless Leader. Serving others in life is like being on a Navy SEAL mission; your journey will take you places you don't know to serve people you don't understand and to solve problems you didn't know existed. And sometimes your mission is so covert that only you will know you were the person behind the victory.

Early in our careers, we tend to get the recognition for the tasks we perform. We get asked to do X, we do it, and we get told, "Good job." The recognition is an extrinsic reward and something we have enjoyed since receiving our first trophy, ribbon, or badge in Little League or Girl Scouts. As we make the decision as a leader to serve others, we are called to be the one rewarding others. We are the ones handing out the ribbons, certificates, and trophies. Servant leaders are the extrinsic givers powered by intrinsic joy when recognizing and applauding others.

Service is bigger than self. Serving others is a calling for the few, the proud, the Fearless Leaders.

How Serving Helps Your Business

When you embrace the idea of serving, you are constantly looking at what you can do for someone else. You use everything you've got to make the world a little better. You keep asking yourself, "How can I help?"

How does this connect to your company? First, think about your mission. Every business must have a clear concept of why they do business. An attitude of serving others should be the foundation for that work, no matter what kind of industry you're in.

Second, people tend to mirror what they see. So when it comes to company culture, when you serve others, your workers will take cues from you. They'll help each other out, collaborate more easily, and keep your mission front and center as a team. Because they understand from you that everyone can contribute and everyone is important, it's much easier to keep office politics from taking over.

Why Is Serving as a Leader So Tough?

With an attitude of service having such clear benefits, you'd think everyone would jump to do it. But the trouble is human nature and our culture can be beasts sometimes. We learn that if we do tasks, we'll get recognized for those jobs, and that feels *amazing*. We like the feeling that we've been noticed and done things right.

Adopting an attitude of service requires us to ditch all that, and instead of always looking to receive, we become the givers. We must stop looking to others to prop up our sense of worth, and that often means we have to do real work to decide what our own values and strengths truly are. If you're not ready to face that work, then serving others on your own or through your company can seem completely out of reach. Service may require you to go places you didn't plan on or to solve problems you hadn't even thought about before. That uncertainty can be scary. But the only anecdote is to be fearless, even in the midst of what's unpredictable or unfamiliar.

The Journey to the Background

When I think about serving as a leader, I can't help but think of the military. Some of the absolute best servants in the U.S. military are the Navy SEALs. What makes them so extraordinary is that they often work extremely covertly. They may be the only ones who know what they contributed to a mission, and they must keep it that way.

Serving as a leader in business is often the same way. The more you provide accolades or resources to others instead of seeking them for yourself, the more you fade into the background. But being "invisible" doesn't mean being unimportant. No one sees the foundation of a house, but if it weren't there, then the whole building would crumble. You are your team's foundation whenever you serve, and the fact that you aren't the person whom others automatically pat on the back is a measure of how well you're doing your job.

> Being "invisible" doesn't mean being unimportant.

Even as a servant, you're still human. You're still going to ask yourself if all the giving is worth it. But when you can tell yourself that you made a positive impact and put your finger on what that impact was, that's when it's clear your service was worthwhile.

You can see the value of serving from your results too. Did you complete your mission according to your values? Is the world closer to what you believe in, either in the way people behave or in what they have available? If the answer is yes, then you met the goal.

Embrace the freedom that serving can provide, and give up the idea that as a founder, executive, or manager, you have to be the one with all the trophies or be the face of the business. Do good things just because it's right and because you can, not because someone is going to put you on a pedestal. As long as *you* know things are not the same as they were because you fearlessly faced yourself and what needed improving around you, you'll pull yourself, your business, and your community in the right direction.

Humility

With victories come all types of rewards, recognitions, and new opportunities. As we discussed earlier, extrinsic rewards are promotions, recognitions, awards, and press clippings. Intrinsic rewards are satisfaction, joy, and motivation for the next opportunity. It's important to experience both. Success is one of the best ways to develop confidence in ourselves. Success is also impactful at removing fear from others and therefore instilling confidence in our friends, family, and colleagues. When you are recognized with an award or press clipping telling the world about your success, that is a good thing, so lean into it.

As a Fearless Leader, your accomplishment is the recognition of you and your team. It will, in turn, instill courage in others who follow you. We live in a world of extrinsic rewards, and to have new opportunities to seize, we sometimes have to receive recognition in order to be known. We've all heard of Mother Teresa, Martin Luther King Jr., and Mahatma Gandhi, and I'm sure we can agree that they were all humble. But their extrinsic recognition for their good work is what propelled each of their missions in life and allowed them to make an exponential impact. There will be times when being recognized for your skill, talent, service, or victory will benefit you directly and times when it will positively serve a bigger purpose in life.

Remember the story I mentioned earlier about when I got promoted to head of sales by our company's vice chairman? Well, while I had started my career as a systems engineer, I eventually found that my real joy was working with customers to solve problems, which meant I needed to transfer to sales so I could be involved in designing new systems and applications to solve business problems. I loved the creativity in it, I enjoyed leading diverse teams, and I especially liked the outcome—you either won or lost—it brought me back to my sports days. I was successful at sales and had, for a few years, received individual sales awards for finishing at the top of the company. I am not really sure why, and I have thought about it a lot, but when I won those sales awards, I stayed pretty humble. I didn't run any victory laps or celebrate in a public way. Maybe it was the fear of whether I would be able to do it again and not slide backward, or maybe it was a lesson from a youth coach. "Say little in defeat and less in victory." Solving problems for the clients, my real passion, coupled with keeping my head small enough to fit through the door, was, I believe, the catalyst behind that big promotion I received. So what am I really saying? Two of my core values—service and humility—were the bedrock behind catapulting my professional career forward.

Serving others for the purpose of being recognized and rewarded, however, is not serving with humility. Balance is the key.

Forty-Nine Years Later, I Met the Man Who Saved My Life

It was in January of 2018 that I noticed a car repeatedly driving past my house. This was unusual for two reasons. First, I live on a quiet street, so cars don't go by all that often. Second, I just had a gut feeling—something about it stood out to me. There was no reason for me to think, at least initially, that it was anything more than someone a little lost and searching for their destination. And even if it was something more sinister, I had no reason to think that I was the target of whoever was in that car.

One day after getting into my own vehicle in preparation to leave the house, I saw the same car out of the corner of my eye, and it was definitely slowing down as it got nearer to my property. In fact, it stopped right in front of my driveway. My thoughts raced. What criminal would approach me so brazenly, or what legitimate business could involve casing my house for weeks? I felt my heartbeat quicken. It was like a vehicular standoff. Who would make the first move? It had to be me, the one who has made a career around the concept of fearlessness.

The window rolled down as I approached the stranger's car. Inside was an older, white, bearded gentleman. I nodded and smiled as I moved closer.

"Do you know who I am?" he asked.

"Santa?" I asked. "You'd be a bit late if so." I felt less nervous now but just as confused.

The man chuckled. "Nope," he said. "I'm Pete Cadwell."

I repeated his name aloud, stalling for time in case some long-buried memory was trying to claw its way up for air. It did sound familiar, but I couldn't seem to place why. "Yep," he replied. "I saved your life when you were born."

My birth date is July 30, 1969. The only problem with that was that my mother's due date was in October. Nonetheless, weighing in at under two pounds, I came into the world a full two months ahead of schedule.

Even with nurses at my bassinet around the clock and doctors massaging my heart to keep it beating, I wasn't expected to make it, which is why, on the day of my birth, I was also baptized, confirmed, and given my last rites. Part of the reason had to do with my mother and me sharing a relatively rare Rh-negative blood type—I needed a lot of it, but there wasn't much available.

My parents were never going to give up, though, and a radio and television campaign was quickly undertaken in the hope of finding willing donors. Miraculously, it did—seven of them, up and down the East Coast. One of them was none other than Pete Cadwell. All of this came rushing back to me on hearing Pete's words.

"Oh my god, Pete," I said. "You were one of my donors!"

He nodded. I felt overwhelmed. I still didn't know why Pete was in my driveway or had chosen now for us to meet, but those things weren't in my mind, just the realization that I was staring at one of the people to whom I literally owed my life. In some jumble of emotional, mixed-up words, I must have managed to ask him what he was doing there.

"You know, Brendan," he said, "I've been driving past your house for about five years now."

I asked him where he lived, now wondering how I could have only noticed in the last few weeks, and his answer—that his home was just down the street—floored me. I recall wondering why Pete had never come by before, and he explained that he'd never felt the need but that he'd seen me playing with my kids, and he knew all about my career. He told me that he'd kept track of me while I was growing up and kept an eye on what was happening in my life.

In any other circumstance, I'm sure I would've been at least a little creeped out. But for some reason, I wasn't. Instead, I was processing how someone could know so much about me when I knew nothing about them and what it must have meant for Pete to be watching me all these years. I was speechless, but once again Pete saved me.

"Something about today," he said. "I just really wanted to stop and talk to you." So we talked. We took a selfie together, and I made it clear he was welcome back anytime. Here was a man who chose to save a stranger's life and ask nothing in return, a man so humble in his kindness that he made me feel special for letting him check in on *me*.

I've gotten a lot of breaks in life. I always try to repay them or pay it forward. I try to be positive, grateful, and fearless because, the way I see it, I've already won just by being here, given the awful odds I started out with.

But Pete gave me another reason to be those things—to be as impactful as I can in the best ways. Because of Pete I'll never forget that the real reason to always strive to be your best self is that you never know who's watching—or how much it might mean to them.

Leadership

Leadership is three simple concepts. The willingness to:

1. Accept responsibility
2. Organize a group of people
3. Achieve a common goal

In the first concept, as a Fearless Leader, you must first accept the responsibility of any situation you are asked or granted to lead; we talked about this in chapter 1. As your Fearless Leadership spreads, the challenges you lead will be tougher, and the opportunities will be greater. You will face increasing degrees of fear, uncertainty, and doubt.

> As individuals we are strong, but as a group, we are limitless.

But you will have built up your fearlessness and prepared for the ever-increasing challenges and opportunities.

In the second concept, Fearless Leaders are organizers of people into a team that is greater than the individuals alone. As individuals we are strong, but as a group, we are limitless. Every year during the off-season of professional sports, I enjoy reading how much better one team has become or how worse another team has gotten. I enjoy it because there are no trophies for the off-season, and very rarely have the best individuals won championships. And this proves the concept of organizing a group of people as a team because teams truly win championships.

And the last concept demonstrates how Fearless Leaders set their sights on a common goal and achieve it through the strength of their team's hyperfocus on that common goal.

How pivotal strong leadership (or the lack thereof) is has never been more clearly laid out than in Leif Babin's account of his overseeing a team of Basic Underwater Demolition/SEAL (BUD/S) training instructors during hell week's formidable boat crew exercise. In his book *Extreme Ownership*, he shares his observations, which I summarize below.

Each crew leader needed to organize a group of people (themselves and a crew of six) to achieve a common goal of winning every boat race. The instructors gave continuous, new, and complicated instructions for each of the crews to complete in competition with each other. Just to give you a peek into the level of challenges these leaders needed to carry their team through, here is an example of instructions for one race: "Paddle your boats out through the surf zone, dump boat, paddle your boats down to the next beach marker, then paddle them back into the beach, run up and over the berm and around the beach marker, then head-carry back to the rope station and then over the berm, and finish here. Got it?"

These were exhausted BUD/S students who are repeatedly dumping themselves into cold water. It is challenging enough to keep yourself motivated to keep going under these circumstances, let alone being responsible to motivate six other team members.

During this particular hell week, Boat Crew II stood out above the rest, winning every race. Morale was high. Boat Crew VI was coming in dead last in every race. The leader and his crew were yelling and accusing each other throughout the exercise. With every race, the losing boat crew was given additional difficulties to perform. The worse they performed, the harder their requirements. Boat Crew VI's team lacked any signs of cohesiveness, and their performance continued to decline. The senior chief decided to take some action and swapped the leaders of the best and the worst crews. No other changes were made. Crew members remained the same, the boat remained the same, and rules and requirements remained the same.

The Boat Crew II leader was less than happy with this change of events, but he accepted the assignment of leader of the worst boat crew with determination. The leader of Boat Crew VI appeared to feel vindicated as he took up his new post. Guess what happened? Boat Crew VI began winning the races. Boat Crew II, a well-built team by their previous leader, continued to perform well, but they were no longer winning every race. In fact, over that first hour of new leadership, Boat Crew VI won the majority of races. They were number one, and gone were the yelling and accusing tones between the crew.

Babin shares that if he hadn't seen such a miraculous and instantaneous transformation with his own eyes, he might have doubted it. This proved a fundamental truth of *Extreme Ownership*: "There are no bad teams, only bad leaders."

Boat Crew II's leader started with accepting responsibility for his first assigned crew and then his second assigned crew. His crew members changed, but his willingness to accept responsibility, organize his crew, and achieve a common goal never wavered. That is Fearless Leadership at its finest.

When First You Lead

My first management job was overseeing an engineering team working on the Pentagon's healthcare systems software. I was twenty-three, and the people I was supervising were between the ages of twenty-eight and fifty-five. Gary was the most senior member of the team with over thirty years of experience, and he was a much better programmer than I was—he used to fix my programs. To say I was intimidated was putting it mildly.

Right out of the gate, I excelled at motivating and creating a fun environment and culture. What I wasn't good at was managing individuals. My style was one size fits all, and I needed to learn that not everybody had to be managed in the same way. Gary didn't need hands-on management; he knew what he was doing. Sarah, who was my age, did need the hands-on approach to get up to speed, and the others needed various approaches in between the two. I began to learn that, as a leader, you need to really know your people.

I was so good at rallying the troops to achieve the goals—a lot of "Let's go, team. We're not stopping for water or sleep—we are taking the hill. Let's go!" So focused on reaching the goal, I'm pretty sure I ran over my soldiers more than once.

Those Friday afternoons when I would be in full motivation mode, telling my team, "We're going to meet Monday's goal. We'll work all weekend to get it done, and I'll bring in pizza!" I can see Gary in the background, when everyone looked to him for help, whispering, "He's on a roll. Just let him play it out." It turned out that the person whom I was most intimidated by was my biggest supporter. Gary would tell me that he was proud of me and that I was going to be a great leader. Eventually, as I got my sea legs, I began to believe it too. As I look back, I'm humbled by my team's patience and support of their young, emerging leader. As young and emerging leaders, we all have so many lessons to learn. As a more seasoned leader today, I am constantly learning new lessons and relying on the wisdom I have acquired through past experiences.

Just Be Good

On day one of my orientation/training week with EDS back in 1991, Jeff Heller, president of the then sixty-thousand-employee company, came to speak to us. He welcomed us all with his smooth Texas drawl, and then he went up to the board and drew a big circle. He said, "These are the values of our clients."

He then drew a circle inside it and said, "These are the values of some of our other clients."

He then put a dot right in the middle and said, "Those are our values at EDS. We must have the most pristine values and perfect values and upright values and core values such that we can serve every one of our clients."

He made a lasting impression on me. I was taught values growing up. I keep my list of values over my desk: strength, courage, faith, service, humility, and leadership. Heller's talk served to reinforce for me how important those values are. The second thing he said was, "Just remember, if you never lie, you never have to remember what you said."

It sounds so simple, but that's what made him so impactful. His overall message was, "You've joined a good company. Just be a good person, and you'll have a great career and an even better life."

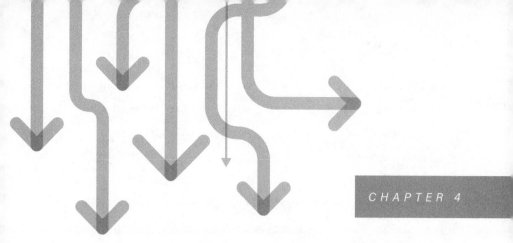

CHAPTER 4

Be Impactful

Making an *impact* in the world, in your community, in a business, and on an individual is one of the most exhilarating feelings you will ever have. And once you've felt it, you don't want it to stop. When you look around, there are certain people who have a knack for making an impact. They join a group at the office, and immediately, the team begins to gain traction. They join a committee for a nonprofit, and the committee's work accelerates. If you don't have that knack naturally, you can develop it. If you do have the knack, you can improve it.

Fearless Leaders bring the six core values we talked about in "Be Good," and they institute the three principles—*vision, goals,* and *productivity*—of "Be Impactful" for consistent performance.

Without a *vision* you won't know where you want to go, and neither will your team. The best way to articulate a vision is through simplicity, connectedness, and storytelling. First, make the vision simple enough for everyone to understand. Second, demonstrate how every role in the company is connected to the vision. If you are challenged to do this as a leader, your teammates will be challenged too. Lastly, create a narrative and bring your vision to life with examples and analogies.

Now a vision is only as good as the work you're willing to put in to achieve it. Setting *goals* that people understand and can execute and align on the actions is a valuable attribute of Fearless Leaders. In fact, achieving goals is what makes the difference between high performance and average performance. Goal alignment and attainment is what separates Fearless Leadership from other forms of transformational theories.

Being *productive* is a vital attribute for successfully achieving your goals. Successful people get stuff done (GSD). We all have the same amount of time in each day—24 precious hours, 1,440 minutes, 86,400 seconds. The people who are most productive have learned how to squeeze the most out of each minute of each day. Some of us are more naturally productive than others. If you have kids, you've seen this firsthand. Some kids do their homework without any parental prodding, while others seem to find distractions easily, and then suddenly, they need parental support to get a project done in time for a fast-approaching deadline. Our professional lives are no different. Some of us get tasks done quickly, and some of us are getting them done just in time for the meeting. Two things I know for sure:

- There is no one right way to be productive.
- The most productive people have a simple system.

I was introduced to the concept of simple systems when I was in elementary school, playing Catholic Youth Organization basketball for St. Chris School. Overall I was an average player, but my free throw shot average was embarrassingly low, and like clockwork every time I stepped up to the throw line, self-doubt took over. I was motivated to get better—because my love of driving to the hoop and making contact is what created my frequent free throw situations in the first place, and I wasn't giving that up—I just didn't know how to get better.

Then one day I was watching a Boston Celtics game, and the great Larry Bird was draining every single free throw attempt. I watched in awe and wished I could shoot like Bird, but what kid didn't want that? A couple of weeks later, I caught an interview with Bird who shared that his free throw shot success was because after practice every day, after everybody else had left, he took one hundred free throw attempts. Talk about a simple system. Starting the next day, I followed Larry's system, and within a month, my free throw average had climbed to over 80 percent. See, it was very simple—just take one hundred shots a day, and your consistency, confidence, and productivity will increase.

Bird's system had a tremendous impact on me. It gave me the tools to make my vision of killing my free throw shot a reality, and it still shapes my belief today that vision + goals + productivity = exponential *impact*.

Vision

When we think of people with vision, we often think about visionaries who have changed the world—Elon Musk, Melinda and Bill Gates, Mother Teresa, and Steve Jobs to name a few. While their visions were all quite different from one another, the exponential impact of each vision is undeniable. Musk's vision for Tesla has revolutionized the auto industry and is making significant impact on our dependence on fossil fuels. The Gates Foundation's vision to eradicate preventable diseases has eliminated polio in India. Mother Teresa's vision to help and advocate for the world's poorest people created 517 missions in over one hundred countries that do just that, and Steve Jobs—well, we all know his vision led to the mobile device that, in today's world, we can't seem to live without.

Every vision doesn't have to save the world. Just like leading, everyone can choose to have a clear vision whether it's for personal development, a community park, or rallying your coworkers to go beyond with every customer. We all have the power to set a vision, share it, and best of all achieve it.

No one is too young to begin to envision their dreams and act on them. Brian Cameron is a great example. I met Brian through my son's lacrosse coach when he was in eighth grade, and I remember, when he was in college, offering him a summer internship at my company if he was interested. His reply was, "Thank you, but my career's going to be in coaching, so that wouldn't be a fit." I was blown away that this young man had such a clear vision for his future *and* knew what he needed (and didn't need) to get there. Brian is now a National Collegiate Athletic Association Division I college lacrosse player at Rutgers.

> No one is too young to begin to envision their dreams and act on them.

That's a dream Brian had envisioned for himself when, at the end of eighth grade, he committed to a lacrosse scholarship with the University of North Carolina. That meant he had to maintain a certain GPA throughout high school and continue to increase his skill as a lacrosse player, all during his teenage years. Talk about needing focus. So how did this thirteen-year-old kid make his college lacrosse dreams come true?

Life is full of constant distractions, and at any given point on any given day, you need to make those little decisions to keep your focus or not. In high school my friends would be going to the movies or just hanging out, and I would have to decide whether I was going to go to the movies—something I will be able to do my whole life—or stick to the goals in front of me now, goals that I only have one chance to get right if I wanted to be a Division I lacrosse player. And now it's pretty cool living the dream that I had when I was thirteen.

When Brian started playing lacrosse in college, he added another vision: to be named an all-American college lacrosse player, something that, today, is very much in his reach. And those distractions he had in high school didn't get any easier in college.

The weekends are the hardest when everybody's going out, partying, and doing different things, and every time, I have to ask myself, "Will that help me get to where I want to be?" which now is an all-American lacrosse player. And if the answer is no, then I shouldn't do it. Obviously, there's a balance, but I want to make sure that all of my decisions are with my goals in mind so that I will eventually achieve my vision. And it's not just about saying no to distractions but it's also about establishing and achieving goals every step of the way. Deciding to eat healthy and stay in top physical shape is one of those daily goals.

When I'm home on winter or summer break, it can be harder to stick to the routine, so in 2013 I founded

Summer Grind. There are a lot of great players who come through New Hampshire, so we established a group chat of, like, twenty kids in the area that are Division I lacrosse players. I'll post in the chat that we're meeting up at the field, and in the beginning, a lot of kids will show up, but eventually, it fizzles down to the five or six kids who are really willing to put in the work day in and day out. We don't make it easy. We write a plan out and just attack it every day, the weight room and lacrosse drills and games up to five hours a day.

Working together on our goals has created a great support system for all of us. We make sure we're keeping each other accountable with nutrition, training, and whatever else we need to do to achieve our dreams. Those are the people I want to surround myself with because people who have bigger goals than me will ultimately push me to be better.

Do you have a vision, and are you holding yourself accountable to it every day? Or maybe you're struggling to define your vision? Here are some tips to get you started.

Create a Personal Vision That Lets You Lead Fearlessly and Drive Success

A clear vision has always been a cornerstone on which people build businesses. You need an understandable, unambiguous concept of what you want others to do and that you can communicate to everyone. Otherwise, trust and effective strategy are just pipe dreams.

To lead fearlessly and overcome doubt, it's critical that your vision is not just clear but also deeply personal and empathetic.

Let's not beat around the bush. Manifesting a vision is hard work. You will have naysayers telling you no or to quit. You will have to overcome the differences that unique experiences and backgrounds create. You will have to figure out all kinds of logistical puzzles, think about ethics, and magically make the ideal supply of resources appear on time. It won't be easy.

So what's going to motivate you through all this? It comes down to your "why" for striving for a better future, a why that has real meaning to you. When you personally understand and crave the change that your vision will bring, then it won't matter how many or how big the obstacles that stand in your way are. You will stand before them with the courage to keep fighting. You will keep pushing for what others say is "unattainable" because your belief that you can and must and that there is no alternative is genuine.

Now you know why it's critical for your vision to be personal, but how do you ensure that you're really connecting the vision to who you are?

1. Define Your Values to Set Your Ground Rules

Everyone has a set of values and philosophies that dictate what they do. The trouble is people can pressure you into compromising your values and philosophies and to act based on what *they* believe. This is why you must solidly connect to your ideals and be willing to stand your ground with kindness. That connection will help you set boundaries and remain true to your vision.

If you're not sure about what your values really are, then look at your habits. Your actions will clue you in about what matters to you. Then aim to be as consistent as you can in the values you prize. If your values need work, change your habits through small steps until you're living the way you want.

2. Stop Focusing So Hard on the Trends

Business professionals are taught that they must pay attention to trends, or they will fail. They must be *agile*. They must be *adaptable*. They must be *flexible*.

While there is truth to those teachings, innovation is arguably the willingness to intentionally toss trends out the window. The motivation of Fearless Leadership cannot be a reed in the wind that bends at every shift or opportunity. The motivation of a Fearless Leader must have staying power. Your why must be something that can drive *you* regardless of the circumstances around you.

Set aside what everyone else says. What is important to *you*? What is so pressing and unique to *your* mind and heart that it keeps you up at night? Those answers are your compass; let them lead you.

3. Pay Attention to Your Emotions

When you truly connect to a dream, the feeling of joy will be so strong that it blocks out fear and erases the word "can't." If you talk about the vision you're trying to build and you don't feel real energy, then you need a new vision, one that speaks to you because if it doesn't, others will be able to tell, and they won't want to follow where you lead.

While no work situation or business will ever be 100 percent perfect, dreams don't feel off, even if others tell you those dreams are impossible. Don't try to force it based on what others tell you it "should" be. Think about and admit which activities lift you the highest. Listen to your gut and use your head to find logical ways to stay oriented toward what makes you happy.

The vision that works best is the one that matters uniquely to you. Any business leader who wants to succeed needs a vision that's personal. It's what allows you to stay motivated no matter what life throws at you. Defining your values, letting go of your death grip on trends, and being hyperaware of what makes you joyful all ensure that you can create a vision that will always have meaning for you. Once you have that vision, share it far and wide with the transparency, confidence, and empowerment others around you are looking for.

Goals

The chicken or the egg? Not everyone starts out with a vision. Sometimes circumstances dictate an action or decision that takes on a life of its own until, suddenly, you realize you're treading water in circles with no clear direction forward. That's how it was for sisters Andi and Danielle when I first met them in 2015.

Our dad owned a delivery business in Boston for thirty years, and when we lost him to cancer in 2012, Andi and I had to decide what to do with the business. Andi was in New York at the time, working in television, and I was home raising three kids, and we just made the decision to go for it. The first three years were a real grind. We just did everything we could to survive.

I agree, it was a grind; the only experience Danielle and I had with the business over the years was delivering packages downtown and answering phones, that sort of thing. We didn't know anything about running a business. Meeting with the accountants and trying to figure out if we were going to make it was an incredible challenge for us. We lost so much business in the beginning, and we were constantly operating from a place of "Let's give it another sixty days." We didn't even know what a profit and loss statement was. We were in day-to-day mode, constantly trying to put out fires. After Brendan began coaching us, we were able to make a real shift from working in the business to working on the business.

Working *in* the business represents the day-to-day "stuff." This includes answering customer calls, managing employees, replying to emails, and more. Working *on* the business is a bit different. It's putting time aside to ask yourself (and your team), "Do I have a strategic plan for my department and my team? Do I have an account plan? Where are we going, and how do we get there?" The results of working *on* the business are marketing and sales plans, professional development day, and account growth strategies—all things that will lead to your business's success. It means get out of the weeds!

It was clear when I met Andi and Danielle that they didn't have a vision for their business. But what they did have in spades was the ability to set goals and execute them. I mean they jump on them. They'll walk out of our strategy meetings, and before they reach the elevator, they're working on their goals. "OK, we have to hire a part-time HR person so we stop making stupid people decisions."

"Yup, I'll take that one. What's next?" And they keep going down the list. They meet every goal. It's super impressive, and their willingness to dig in and make it happen is what motivates me to keep coaching them. They are real, they are authentic, they own their development, and they are the best.

Brendan was the first person, besides our immediate family, who believed we could do this, and that gave us confidence. He helped us step back and look at the bigger picture and ask, "What are our goals?" For us it's continuing to grow successfully. Now that we know where we want to go, we've learned to set smaller goals to help us get there. Every time we met those early goals, it gave us confidence to set another one. Every milestone we achieved was motivation to go further. In year two our revenue was a little over the million-dollar mark. In year ten our revenue is over a million a month. One of the reasons we've reached that milestone is we've learned to grow with our customers. We always serviced eastern Massachusetts and southern New Hampshire, and then when our largest account told us they were expanding into New Jersey, Andi and I were like, "No, we can't do it."

Brendan helped us break it down into actionable goals, and we did it and more. We've entered five new states as a result of building confidence one state at a time. And that confidence has trickled down to our employees, whom we now encourage to set their own goals. This is possible now because everyone knows where we are headed and how to get there.

This goes back to working on the business where all the employees see our strategic plan, our vision, and our goals. That aligns us and allows us to grow and develop as a company.

Why Set Goals?

The first time a runner sets their sights on running a marathon, no matter how clearly and passionately they envision running across that finish line, they know it isn't going to happen tomorrow or the next day or even the next month. They will have to build their endurance mile by mile until they are mentally and physically capable of running twenty-six miles—they set goals, stepping-stones if you will, to reach their vision. Without them they will never cross the finish line.

Goals give you

- long-term vision to help guide you toward your purpose,
- short-term accomplishments to keep you motivated and inspired,
- focus to reach your potential,
- ability to organize your time and resources,
- measurable progress and accountability to keep you on track, and
- confidence to set new, bigger goals.

By now I'm sure it's clear that I am a goal-setting enthusiast. I have been as long as I can remember. In fact, I have a file with all my annual goals from 1990 to today, and I always have my current year goals tacked up on my wall. I love looking back on my goals and seeing how they have evolved through my life. The early ones are straightforward: graduate from a good college, get married, and have kids. And as I achieved those goals, my vision and subsequently my goals shifted. How can I be the best parent to my kids? How can I positively impact others? Those became the types of questions that drove my vision and goals.

What didn't change is my goal-setting and execution process. Here are some tips and techniques to help you get started or perhaps fine-tune your own process.

- Define your SMART goals, a goal-setting criterion attributed to Peter Drucker's "management by objectives" approach as outlined in his book *The Practice of Management*. Write down the *main* things you aim to accomplish. Make sure they are as follows:
  - *S*pecific: Be Focused and Clear
    - Your goal must be clear and well defined.
    - Your goals need to show you the way. Make it as easy as possible to get where you want to go by defining where you want to end up.
  - *M*easurable: Use Numbers and Choose a Goal You Can Track
    - Include precise time, amounts, and dates so you can measure your degree of success and celebrate the wins.
  - *A*chievable: Stretch, but Stay within Reach
    - Make sure it's a goal that you can achieve, but resist the urge to set goals that are too easy.
    - Your goals should challenge you to raise the bar.
  - *R*elevant: Relate to Your Vision
    - Keep your goals consistent with the direction you want your career and life to take.
  - *T*ime-Based: Set Deadlines, Timelines, and Checkpoints
    - Your goals must have deadlines providing you a sense of urgency and the opportunity to celebrate your successes along the way.

- Develop your goals.

- From the list of things to accomplish, write three primary goals.
- Write up to ten-word descriptions of each goal.
- Develop two to four actions to support each goal.

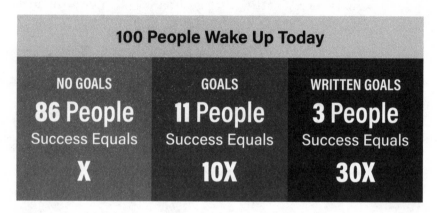

Now you have your personal goal bible—fantastic! By formulating a goal-driven plan and *writing* it down, you've joined the 3 percent. Welcome to the club. Now the real work begins: take action. Let's look at how you can increase your productivity and GSD by establishing a simple system.

Be Productive by Keeping It Simple

Keep it *simple*. As humans with powerful brains, it's no surprise that we tend to overthink, overdesign, and overcomplicate things. Think about Larry Bird's free throw success—one hundred shots a day after practice, that's it. No discussion on spin of the ball, hand placement, shooting with your legs, focusing on the back of the rim, none of it—just daily repetition to build muscle memory and instill confidence.

The best business example of keeping it simple that I can think of is Amazon, the e-commerce giant that has made it so easy to buy stuff. From their one-click checkout to buttons in your pantry to subscription services to next-day delivery, shopping has never been simpler. And how have we responded to Amazon's simplistic ways? We've made them one of the most valued companies and brands in the world.

So why is it so hard for other companies to follow their blueprint for success? That's simple to answer—ease of use and simplicity are built into the DNA of Amazon, whereas competitors may copy a new, convenient feature but then fall back to their familiar, complex ways.

How can you translate the simplicity of Amazon to Fearless Leadership? You guessed it: build a system that makes it simple for others to follow you, to understand you, to communicate with you, to be your friend, to be your neighbor, or to work for you or alongside you. At the core of being simple are three things: a vision or purpose people can relate to, a repeatable and consistent system, and a relentless attitude of keeping it simple.

There's no doubt that keeping it simple can be a challenge. You get a group of adults together, and something simple can become oh so complicated. Announcing that pizza will be delivered for lunch will ignite an avalanche of suggestions on the best time to have it delivered, what types of pizzas should be ordered, and where and what time everyone should eat it. It's just pizza, people—either you eat it or you don't!

Spaghetti with a Side of Marshmallow, Please

Peter Skillman's spaghetti tower design challenge is a great example of how we get in our own way when trying to find a solution. Skillman's challenge was for each group of four to build the tallest possible structure using the following items:

- twenty pieces of uncooked spaghetti

- one yard of transparent tape
- one yard of string
- one standard-size marshmallow

The only rule was that the marshmallow had to end up on the top of the tower. Skillman has performed this challenge all over the world with business students, engineers, and kindergartners. The business students jumped right into strategy. They engaged in an examination of the materials and an exchange of ideas, coming up with several options. Skillman describes their process, "It was professional, rational, and intelligent." The engineers were "solid, didn't game the system. They were efficient and methodical." With both groups, tasks were divvied up, and they got to work.

The group of kindergarteners did not strategize, exchange ideas, or examine the items. They simply began building. Standing close together, they grabbed items back and forth between them while shouting sporadically, "Here!"

"No, here!"

Skillman describes them as "trying a bunch of stuff."

Guess which group had the greatest success. In dozens of trials, the kindergartners built structures that averaged twenty-six inches tall. The lowest-scoring groups, the business students, erected ones that were a mere ten inches tall.[12]

The kindergartners kept it supersimple. It wasn't the level of skill of the participants that mattered; it was how they interacted with each other. The good news is we can learn to keep it simple too. And I can only imagine if you tried this exercise with a group of CEOs.

---

12   Peter Skillman Design, accessed April 26, 2022, http://www.peterskillmandesign.com/#/spaghetti-tower-design-challenge/.

How to Build a Simple System That Skyrockets Your Productivity

Write things down. You can use good old paper and pencil, Post-its, a digital app, or whatever works for you. The simple act of writing things down longhand is important for any productivity system. It can make recall easier and help you sort through your thoughts and organize them in a way others can more easily follow.

Create an action list. This is really your to-do list. The traditional to-do list has gained a negative connotation, as it can become overwhelming and take on a life of its own. Call it an action list instead. This simple relabeling will remind you that *you* are in charge. The word "action" signifies progress on a journey toward something rather than just checking off an individual task.

Prioritize actions. You'll have items on your action list that are more important than others. Ask yourself what your self-driven vision really is and prioritize the actions that are most critical to obtaining it. Those that don't make the priority list may still be beneficial, so don't toss them out just yet. But if they are not directly on the path to your main goal, then move them to the bottom of your action list.

Many individuals have great ambition, integrity, and influence, which are all essential leadership traits, but if they don't know exactly what they want to do and what's necessary to do it, those traits alone won't get them to the top. Top performers create a customized system that will help them move cleanly from one step to the next with good self-accountability and consistency.

Lean on the three tips above to create a system that's ideal for you. The clearer you are on what you have to work with and where you want to go, the faster you'll walk across your personal finish line.

By sharing a clear vision, setting achievable goals, and increasing productivity by establishing a simple system and empowering others to follow it, you will make an *exponential* impact on the world.

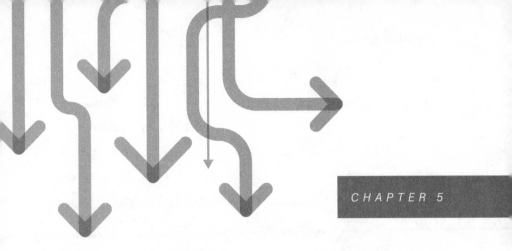

CHAPTER 5

Be Collaborative

Now that you know what you want to achieve as a leader, the question becomes *how* you are going to achieve your vision. A Fearless Leader doesn't go it alone. They build strong teams and leverage the collective power of those teams. How? Collaboration.

Collaboration requires a continuous and conscious effort to reach beyond yourself and connect with others. Collaboration is reciprocal. It doesn't work if a leader only directs and pushes information, ideas, lessons, and experiences out. A Fearless Leader must also accept direction, information, ideas, lessons, and experiences *in* from those around them. In fact, they must go a step further and actively seek out the advice, ideas, and lessons of others. There are five key tools that a leader must employ if they are to create a collaborative environment that will make their vision a reality: *brand, relationships, communication, emotional quotient,* and *influence*.

Know who you are. As you go through your life's journey, there is only one thing you will leave this world with, and that is your reputation. Your reputation is your *brand*. Ever listen closely to a eulogy? You will hear about someone's life and their accomplishments, and if you listen attentively, you will know their reputation: their *brand*.

Fearless Leaders build a brand that is rock solid because that is the foundation others come to depend on. Your brand is who you are. When others know who you are and when they believe in your brand, positive connections and interactions will develop, building the base for solid relationships.

Leadership is about organizing a group of people. People require your time, energy, focus, and investment. Fearless Leaders develop *relationships* and take the required time to invest in those relationships. Fearless Leaders are also willing to put themselves out there and network, meet new people, and connect more often. Sometimes this can be scary because fear, uncertainty, and doubt creep in. But you are developing the attributes and a leadership approach that push past that and build a tribe of people who want to follow your fearless style.

In order to convey their brand and build relationships, Fearless Leaders must *communicate* with clarity, transparency, and authenticity. Developing your communication attributes is vital to instilling confidence in your audience and removing their fear, uncertainty, and doubt. Communication is all-encompassing: it's how you speak, how you write, how you listen, and how you interact.

How well you communicate with those you lead will be directly impacted by your *emotional quotient* (EQ). High achievers and performers have the intelligence quotient (IQ) to achieve their goals and be leaders. But Fearless Leaders develop the far more important aspect of intelligence known as EQ, the ability to identify and manage one's own emotions, as well as the emotions of others. This is perhaps the toughest Fearless Leader attribute to develop, but it is also one that will get you the farthest in your life. In fearful moments when doubt and uncertainty enter the landscape, your EQ will be the lifeline others depend on, the voice they listen to, the rock they cling to, and the Fearless Leader they follow.

Each of the attributes outlined—brand, relationships, communication, and emotional quotient—play a role in establishing your *influence* across your family, friends, colleagues, and community.

Brand

PlayHardLookDope, that's a brand name that will grab your attention and stick with you. It did with me when I came across the store in SoHo back in 2017. That's when I met owners Jon Nelsen and Ebony Mackey, and it was clear that PlayHardLookDope wasn't just a catchy name; it was the authentic lifestyle of Jon and Ebony. They live their brand. They honor their brand. They are their brand.

> When we decided to brand our idea for the type of jewelry we wanted to design and sell, we knew that it would have to coincide with the lifestyle that we live because we weren't going to give that up. We have a strong belief in having fun, in being transparent, in styling, and in products that are sustainable and accessible.

Like many businesses in the pandemic, PlayHardLookDope was forced to adjust and adapt. Their adjustments were wildly successful, and they did it without any compromise to their brand. After they had to close the SoHo store, they were given a two-week opportunity around the holidays to set up a couple of tables in front of a vacant store in the exclusive Westchester Mall.

We live in Hell's Kitchen in New York City. We knew nothing about Westchester, nothing. But when the offer was made to come check out the space and see if we wanted it, we biked to the train, rode for several stops, and then biked the rest of the way to meet the woman who had reached out to us. Now Jon is always the "let's do it and figure it out as we go" kind of guy. I am more cautious and think about how we are going to do it and about the what-ifs. But we both knew we had to do this.

For two weeks we commuted to Westchester, lugged two heavy tables in and out of the vacant store every day, and set up our display. We had no idea what to expect in this high-end mall where all the stores were national brands. But we killed it. The feedback that we received from the mall shoppers was that we were offering something different, that the mall had become just more of the same—and we were definitely not that!

That fearless leap led to more success.

At the end of the two weeks, Ebony wondered if they would rent us the store space. I told her that I didn't think so since we would be the only non-national brand, but what the hell, I'll ask.

They offered us a deal. We negotiated. And we set up shop. Since we were not a national brand, they had the right to kick us out with a thirty-day notice. We made the store look so cool inside and fashionable and very aesthetically pleasing that within six months, one of the national brands located in a smaller store wanted our space. We had to vacate, but the mall offered us another space, one that was four thousand square feet, which was crazy huge—three times the size of our current space and double the rent, double the electric, more inventory, more fixtures, just more of everything.

We couldn't fill up four thousand square feet with just jewelry, so I decided we'd add apparel that fit with our PlayHardLookDope brand to help fill the space. We went and bought a machine printing press and started printing graphics on clothing in the store.

Jon's never-be-afraid-to-fail attitude has paid off with their highly successful flagship store.

When I think about our brand, we take whatever comes and make it work the best we can for us while continuing to protect our brand. When Jon and I decided to make the move to the Westchester Mall—which is so different from our SoHo location—our vibe, our style, how we set our space, all of that stayed the same. We don't try to blend in. We're different. That's part of our brand. And I think that speaks to our customers. They want to look different, feel different, and still be able to wear our product in their everyday life. That's what they've come to expect.

Jon and Ebony's unique and memorable brand stuck with me, and as the COVID-19 pandemic started to slow down and we were having our employees come back to the office, I wanted to get every team member something really cool to commemorate coming through this crisis together. Throughout this time, we launched Project COOL, we refused to use the word "COVID-19," and as I thought of who the coolest people I knew were, Jon and Ebony immediately came to mind. Fast-forward through a few Zoom calls, together we made every employee a custom COOL bracelet, with each stone having significant meaning to our vision and values as a company. A year later as I walk the building, I still see so many people wearing Jon and Ebony's jewelry.

Three Cornerstones to Building Your Brand

What does your brand say about you? Does it instill confidence, or does it instill uncertainty? Whatever your brand is today, you can improve it, enhance it, and establish it as a calming influence in a storm. A truly Fearless Leader makes everyone in the room feel a tad more comfortable simply because they are there. As you continue to build and improve your brand, consider the following three ways to make it the best possible:

Be Authentic: Make sure your brand represents who you are and who you are striving to be. Embrace your personality, your attributes, and your strengths and channel your energy into developing that brand. Your first step in doing this is increasing your self-awareness of what that authentic brand is, and we will chat more about that when we dive into EQ.

Be Passionate: Build your brand around your passion. If you love animals or are creative and artistic or love sports, whatever you are excited and motivated by, make it part of your brand. If your brand includes your passions, you will absolutely build it faster and with more authenticity. Why? Because it represents who you are and what you love, and that passion will shine through to those you are leading.

Be Tangible: Reputations and brands are built on actions, not words. Inevitably, what you do is who you are. What you don't do is also who you are. If you always follow through, your reputation is one of trust and dependability. If you seldom follow through, your brand screams unreliable. Simply saying who you are and what you're about isn't going to cut it.

When people think of you, they will think of the tangible things they know about you—you love animals and volunteer at the pet shelter, you are creative and play the piano, you love athletics and coach youth soccer. See the connection between your passion and your tangible action? Bring your authentic self to your passions for all the world to see.

Building a solid brand and reputation is a choice you can make today. Growing your brand and reputation is a long journey. The good news is you are in control over how people see you. Make the choice to work authentically, passionately, and tangibly, and you'll gain the fearless attitude that helps every great leader establish a successful reputation.

> What you do is who you are. What you don't do is also who you are.

Relationships

Early in my career, I thought I was pretty good at building relationships. As I grew in my career and wanted to become a better leader, I realized that I was good at creating relationships but not so good at investing the time to nurture ongoing relationships. We've all gotten the call, text, or email out of the blue from a past relationship asking how we are doing, followed by, "Can you do me a favor?"

One day I realized I was that past relationship reaching out and asking that question. That's when I made a conscious decision to do my best to put in the necessary time and effort to nurture my relationships. It's not easy. Most of us are always looking for ways to stretch time and fit more into our day, and sometimes that feels impossible. But it's important to commit to making the time and the investment to the relationships that are right for you no matter how challenging.

In the tech age, most of us have been conditioned to think that the more relationships we have, the better. We brag about the size of our networks and work hard to connect on social media. But when push comes to shove, not all relationships have the same weight. Some are more important than others. The trick is to know which ones are the most valuable and to invest in those relationships *with purpose*.

Admittedly, I've made missteps in this arena. For example, when my wife and I were getting ready to celebrate my fiftieth birthday a few years back, she asked me to throw together a list of people I wanted to take on a trip with us. When she seemed surprised at some of the names I spit out, I stepped back and thought about how I picked everyone. The truth was some of the people I was going to invite, while I enjoyed spending time with them, weren't the most valuable to me. They hadn't been involved with me through the most meaningful points in my life.

I looked at that birthday list again. This time I thought about who had had the biggest influence on me at every stage of my life—as a kid, during college, or when I first started as a professional. The types of people on my *new* list were all over the map, and when I got back in touch with them, we picked up right where we left off. That was only possible because I had real friendships with those people, deep relationships with them; they weren't acquaintances passing through my life. I knew that from that point on, those were the relationships I needed to put my energy and resources into. So my list wasn't "who was in my life on my fiftieth birthday?" but it was who had made the biggest impact over my lifetime. And it made for one pretty eclectic group of people from all walks of life, but it also truly represented my journey through life instead of simply a moment.

Of course, you don't have to wait until your next birthday to figure out which relationships matter the most to you. It's something you can figure out right now, today.

Eight Keys to Investing in Your Relationships with Purpose

Investing in the right people helps you personally. These people keep you calm. They build your confidence. They make you feel like you belong and that you matter. You can't always choose to get rid of other stressors, but you can choose who you want to be your friends and business partners/mentors. If you choose wisely, then happiness gets a whole lot closer.

Investing in the right relationships can have amazing payoffs for your career or business. It can mean that you get the right advice when you need it, your access to resources is reliable, and you get in on the ground floor with new projects. The old saying that it's not *what* you know but *who* you know is often true. So don't just throw a dart at the wall and hope for the best. Consciously choose the people you want to give to and take with you for the long haul and go all in. It might be a much smaller circle than you were convinced you needed, but that circle is going to prove to be incredibly solid as you build the fearless life you want. Here are some steps to help you get started.

1. Identify Influential People around You

Think about who your *external influencers* are. These are the people in your business sphere including clients, prospects, and partners. Who among them are the achievers, the ones who share your motivation, and the ones you admire and want to learn from?

Then there are your *internal influencers* in business, the leaders, colleagues, and collaborators whom you interact with on a regular basis. Who are you drawn to work with and who encourages you to stretch in new ways and helps you get stuff done?

What does your *personal sphere of family and friends* look like? Who believes in you, supports you, and encourages you every step of the way? Equally important, who in your group of family and friends needs your support and encouragement? Who inspires you? Who has achieved a goal you are reaching for?

Who sits in your *social sphere*? This is a larger group of networking and community groups. The next time you attend a networking event or meeting, look through the lens of "Who are my potential long-term collaborators, leaders, mentors, and mentees? Who can help me grow?"

2. Be a Good Listener

You've identified the relationships that you want to invest in with purpose; now it's time to up your listening game. It's time to silence your phone, put it aside, and actively listen. Active listening requires that you provide the person who's speaking your full attention. Maintain eye contact and positive body language. Ask about what they care about and what excites and motivates them and *remember their responses*. Follow up, follow up, follow up. Emails are OK, texts are good, phone calls are better, handwritten notes are meaningful, and the unexpected is the best. No matter how you choose to follow up, just do it. Don't wait to run into them or for them to reach out to you. Be proactive.

3. Be Visible and Work Hard

Be available, be present, and help before you are asked. If follow-up is key to good listening, follow-through is key for your actions: do what you say you are going to do and more. Roll up your sleeves and work hard in your industry and your community. Show people what you're made of, and opportunity will follow.

4. Intend to Give

While you are looking for relationships that help you grow, the primary goal of developing purposeful relationships is not to get but to give. Enter every relationship knowing what you have to offer—your gratitude, time, attention, knowledge, experience, connection, energy, and commitment. Make a list of all you have to offer and keep adding to it.

5. Be Yourself

In all your relationships, stay true to who you are. Yes, relationships make you grow and adapt, but they should never require you to change your values. If they do, they're not the right relationship for you. The strongest relationships are the ones in which you can be yourself. Building and nurturing relationships is hard work, but if you're willing to put in the time, to learn new things, and to step outside of your comfort zone, creating a sphere of strong relationships will be well worth the effort.

Communicate

Most of the great businesses of the world have great services and products. That's a given. What really makes them stand out is that their leaders are fantastic communicators. These leaders teach others how to communicate well too so that connection becomes a cornerstone for the culture of the entire organization. But what exactly is it that makes Fearless Leaders' communication stand out? It's not necessarily eloquence. You don't have to be Shakespeare for people to pay attention. It's not even assertiveness when talking to a large group of people that makes them stand out. Some of the most profound communication that leaders offer happens as a quiet gift to just one person in times of hurt and need. And this is enhanced by the four main traits Fearless Leaders have that make their communication effective.

The first trait of fearless communication is having a clear message, one that you've established through the development of your vision and goals.

The second trait is knowing who you're delivering the message to—know your audience. Do they want more or less—in person, email, text, or video communication—or do they want you to listen first? As you get opportunities to communicate as a leader, take time to prepare and think about what the audience wants and needs. Do they need you to bring high energy or calming energy, do they want facts or feelings, and are they looking for a long explanatory communication or a short and snappy one? The more you invest in knowing your audience, the more they will invest in listening to the message.

In business you have relationships with customers, with employees, with vendors, and more. Each one of those relationships is different and requires varying nuances in how you communicate with each group and individual within that group while staying true to your *brand*—your reputation.

Jon and Ebony shared how their different leadership styles provide them a balanced approach to communicating their brand.

I work more closely with the staff. When Jon learns of something that an employee has done that he doesn't like, he'll want to immediately shoot off a blunt email. And I'll be like, "It's okay. I'll deal with it." I've worked in retail, and I want to do everything that is opposite of the things I did not like, which means I want to make anybody who works for us in the store or behind the scenes of the brand feel comfortable, to enjoy what they are doing, and to not feel like we have our thumb on them all the time.

Things happen in everyone's life—missing the bus, oversleeping—and I just need to be the one to give it a little bit of a soft touch. Jon is the CEO, and that's a very different mindset. He's also always confident that anyone can do anything, and that can be intimidating for some of the staff who don't have his confidence. So I'm the gentle human resource person. But when it comes to problems with a customer, Jon is usually the gentler communicator.

I will definitely bend over backward to help a customer in ways that Ebony won't. If a customer comes in and they've damaged their piece of jewelry in some way, even if they've had it over a year, I will always offer to repair it. I think that's how we've built such a great client base.

I'm more like, "They bought it over a year ago. They damaged it. They need to take responsibility." Jon will always—always—take care of them, no questions asked. It helps that we contrast each other and know who's the best communicator for the situation.

One thing they both agree on is that no one should be treated rudely—that doesn't fit their brand. Retail is known for their occasional rude customers, and while many businesses state that the customer is always right, that isn't true for PlayHardLookDope.

> No one's always right. When your business is in a mall full of high-end corporate brands that have a code of conduct that says the customer is always right and a customer goes in the store next to you and loses their mind, gets their way, and then comes into Play-HardLookDope and think they can behave that way here, we're like, "No, no, this is different." We are real people; our staff are real people. We're going to protect them. We're going to protect us. We want our brand to influence people to be a good person, and sometimes that means clearly communicating that standard to our customers even if that means we may lose their business.

The third trait of fearless communication is transparency. This just means sharing your expertise or the information you have in a straightforward but kind way, including what's going on in the company. You don't try to sugarcoat anything, and you comfort people when they need it. When you only tell part of the story, your audience will make up the other part, and that can be dangerous, spreading fear and doubt. Get comfortable saying "I don't know" because sometimes you just don't.

And the fourth trait of fearless communication is to be authentic. Be yourself; don't try to be someone you are not. Show your personal truths and admit what you like or don't like, the mistakes you make, and again what you don't know. Share what drives you. Even though you may need to adjust your approach to different situations, the company potluck is a lot different from a formal fundraiser; for example, being authentic means your overall style stays consistent. There's no faking it or pretending for appearances.

> Get comfortable saying "I don't know" because sometimes you just don't.

When people know what to expect from you, it's easier for them to give you their trust. They won't have a problem confiding in you or sharing their ideas with you because they know you'll be genuine, and they don't get the sense that something is off. The dynamic duo sisters I talked about earlier, Andi and Danielle, lead their company as co-CEOs in the most authentic way. Their teams know they stepped in for their dad, and this wasn't their big plan, and they were honest about that as they started running the company. As they embraced being the company's leaders, worked on their business, and built their plans and confidence, their teams viewed them differently as well. But all along the way, Andi and Danielle stayed true to who they were and always were the most authentic people you could ever meet.

Communication Takes Work, But the Harvest Is Golden

Of course, this isn't the end of the story. Once you have these four key communication ingredients going, you still have work to do. Pay attention to whether your message is clear and consistent over time. Think about pacing and knowing how much communication is enough. Develop a sense of what the ramifications of your communications are going to be for better or worse. This all takes critical thinking skills, objectivity, and a heightened awareness of facts and culture.

Approach communicating fearlessly from multiple angles and accept that it doesn't just happen with a snap of your fingers. Work at it with intention and see it as a constant work in progress. The same characteristics that make your communication successful— a clear message, knowing your audience, transparency, and being authentic—go beyond improving business results and productivity. They enable real friendships. If your company is truly about serving others, then that's the real gold. Let this shine and don't hold back. When you have solid relationships strengthened by outstanding communication, everything else will follow naturally.

Emotional Quotient (EQ)

We've all been in a situation when we were shocked by someone's inability to read the room, and they make a statement or behave in a way that triggers negative emotions in those around them with no chance of a positive outcome. When I think of someone with a low EQ, I can't help but think of the *Seinfeld* crew. In season 7's final episode, "The Invitations," George laments his engagement to Susan but doesn't want to endure the fight that will ensue if he calls the wedding off. His friends Elaine and Kramer suggest he take up smoking since his fiancée hates that or that he should offend her by asking her to sign a prenuptial agreement. All these characters are in their thirties, but their emotional intelligence has never risen beyond that of an adolescent. Susan dies, George is off the hook, and he calls another woman, tells her his fiancée just died, and asks her out on a date. The woman, being the only one in the episode with a modicum of EQ, abruptly hangs up on him, leaving George dumbfounded.

So isn't that quite the low-EQ example? In fact, isn't it quite abrupt and superficial, and doesn't it really sidestep everything we have been talking about as Fearless Leaders? Well, I could have picked any of hundreds of examples from *Seinfeld*, but this one takes the cake, and I am not implying wedding cake either!

So what exactly is EQ? Emotional quotient is your ability to be aware of your emotions, the emotions of others, and the ability to use that awareness to guide your behavior and the behavior of others in a positive way. Let's talk about each of those in more detail.

You can't have a healthy EQ without self-awareness. Take time to recognize what triggers your feelings, be that excitement, anxiety, energy, lethargy, satisfaction, unfulfillment, happiness, sadness, anger, or any other emotions that well up on you. Stop for a minute and pick five of those feelings and write them down on a piece of paper. Now think of a few things in life that trigger those feelings. Simply by doing this exercise, you are becoming more self-aware.

Through her work as an executive coach, Tasha Eurich, organizational psychologist and author of *Insight: The Surprising Truth about How Others See Us, How We See Ourselves, and Why the Answers Matter More than We Think,* came to see self-awareness not just as an important skill but also an essential one. Through her research the skill of self-awareness proved itself to be the foundation for high performance, smart choices, and lasting relationships.

Self-awareness is not just confined to being aware of our own values and personality strengths and weaknesses (internal self-awareness) but it also requires us to have an awareness of how others see us (external self-awareness). The two don't always match up. While you may have a low external self-awareness, you can still have a high internal self-awareness and vice versa. Let me share with you the external self-awareness wake-up call my executive coach gave me.

"Hi, Brendan. I've really been looking forward to meeting you. As your executive coach, I've interviewed the people you work for, and they really love you. They say you overdeliver on everything you promise to achieve. The people who work for you really enjoy working for you. You're a good leader."

"Great," I said, beaming.

"I also interviewed your colleagues across departments that you work with. What do you think they think of you?" he asked.

"That I'm great to work with." I laughed.

"Not exactly," he said.

This was a game-changing moment for me. As my executive coach walked me through the responses of my colleagues and what they meant, I began to see that in my narrow focus on leading my team and delivering as promised to the higher-ups, I neglected to invest in my colleagues across the aisle. Here I was the head of sales, and I wasn't spending the time needed with the head of marketing or strategy. Now when I look back, it's a no-brainer, but as a younger executive, I needed a coach to slow me down and walk me through how important peers are to my own success in the company and how I can cultivate them. I began having monthly meetings with related department heads, and it really changed my whole approach and perspective on leading through collaboration.

I'm not alone in having my self-awareness blind spots. In fact, Eurich's research revealed that while 95 percent of us believe we are self-aware, the truth is that number is closer to 15 percent. That means 80 percent of us have a bit of work to do. The good news is that self-awareness, like the many attributes of leadership, is a skill everyone can develop. I shared a quick exercise above to help you hone your internal self-awareness skill, and you can do the same with your external self-awareness: get vulnerable and ask those around you for honest feedback on your interactions *and* be willing to openly receive and examine that feedback. It's a little scary putting yourself out there, but as the Fearless Leader you were meant to be, I know you can do it.

Being aware of your emotions and what triggers those emotions is the first step of developing your EQ. Once recognized, it's time to develop your ability to intelligently self-manage your emotions. Reflect on an instance when someone made you feel upset, angry, or unfulfilled. How did you handle that situation? Were you able to process it successfully and have a productive day, or did it eat you up inside and impact how you reacted with others throughout your day?

EQ also requires a level of social awareness. How's your perception of the emotions, triggers, reactions, and interactions of the people around you? How do your emotions and actions trigger positive or negative emotions in others? While you can't refrain from sharing bad news, you can manage your delivery and its impact on others. Be empathetic to why that news will have a negative impact and how you can help others manage it. You can also choose to trigger positive emotions in others by acknowledging their good work, encouraging them to share their ideas, and getting to know what's important to them.

Achievers and high performers have the intelligence, IQ, to achieve their goals and be leaders. Fearless Leaders intentionally develop their *emotional quotient* to give them the staying power to achieve their vision through high performance, smart choices, and lasting relationships.

Developing your EQ is a work in progress, and you won't always get it right. For me I am aware when a day or a meeting or specific people are going to trigger me in a negative way, and I focus on how I can rise up and not let them or the situation get the better of me. I repeat two things to myself when I am entering a "hot zone":

1. "Small things amuse small minds, so just let it go and be the bigger person."
2. "The only way they can win is if you let them. So win the day!"

Now I can't tell you I am always the bigger person or that I always win the day, but I can tell you I try like heck! In fact, come visit me in my office, and I can show you these two sayings in a frame on my desk hidden from open view but in my line of sight— they sit there as reminders to myself because I know I'm still very much a work in progress.

Influence

We can't talk about influence without addressing the phenomenon that is social media influencers. Social media has ushered in a whole new world of affecting change on a massive scale. From women demonstrating how to put on makeup to film producers to fashion bloggers, all have amassed millions of followers. I'm fascinated by the phenomenon where people who often start out offering advice or entertainment from their kitchen table build up their followers to a point in which sponsors, vendors, and engine sites are paying them to grow their followership, and in some cases, their significant following leverages into multimillion-dollar businesses. This platform can be a powerful opportunity to influence society. I'm going to talk about two of the top ten Instagram influencers today, Huda Kattan (known on Instagram as hudabeauty) and Zach King.

Kattan, a professional makeup artist, decided to start a beauty blog, HudaBeauty.com, in 2010, then added a Huda Beauty YouTube channel and Instagram account shortly after. By 2013 Kattan decided to create a collection of false eyelashes under the Huda Beauty brand.

Today Huda Beauty's Instagram account has 46.8 million followers, and in 2020 Forbes ranked Kattan as one of America's Richest Self-Made Women that year with an estimated net worth of $510 million. That's an opportunity to influence almost 50 million people!

Huda uses her influence to encourage women to embrace their natural beauty and to challenge beauty and fashion companies to stop photoshopping everyone into what their ideal of what they think beauty should be.

"I've been in this space for a long time, and I've felt sooo much pressure myself to edit my pictures and to try to fit into this online idea of the perfect body. Let me tell you, there's no such thing as the perfect body or the perfect face. You are beautiful in your own way, do what makes you feel happy and what makes you feel beautiful." The responses from her followers suggest that her positive message is having impact.

Now let's talk about former Vine creator Zach King. When King didn't get into film school as he had hoped in 2012, he and his partner, Aaron, began working out of their garage to make fun YouTube videos for Zach's YouTube channel, Final Cut King, and Aaron's YouTube channel, VFX Bro. Today Zach has a combined social reach of over 105 million followers and his company, King Studio, has partnered with brands such as Disney, Apple, Sony, Nike, and Coca-Cola.

Zach uses his influence to encourage people to find their creativity, and on the personal side, he shares what it means to be a dad and the role he and his wife have chosen as foster parents—the opportunity to positively influence 105 million people![13]

We're not all going to influence 100 people, let alone 100 million, but we can all be influential one person at a time. So what makes one

---

13   The Zach King Team, accessed August 30, 2022, https://www.zachkingteam.com/about.

person more influential than another? What makes people listen to a particular voice or opinion over another's? Let's look at three methods to increase your influencing skills.

Influence through Inquiry vs. Advocacy

I learned the art of influencing through inquiry vs. advocacy when I faced a challenging experience during a board meeting for an organization. There was no doubt that every one of us was passionate about the mission of the organization, but there was a decision before us and a difference of opinion. A fellow board member and I advocated our positions. I went first. Once the floor was my colleague's, she went on the attack. I now saw her as my opponent, my walls went up, and I shut down. I was confused. Weren't we on the same team? Didn't we have the same goal? Yes, we slightly disagreed on how to accomplish it, but I had no idea how this difference of opinion turned into a duel. I looked to another board member for assistance, guidance, something, and he obliged. His points were aligned with mine, but he managed to neutralize the tension *and* persuade everyone in the room to consider his perspective in a way that I hadn't. In the end, even my opponent agreed that our approach made the most sense.

How had this happened? When I asked this question of a wise man I know, he told me simply, "Well, your supporting colleague took a completely different approach. You *advocated*. He *inquired*." And he set about explaining the difference between the two. He defined both approaches and gave me tips on how to include inquiry in my repertoire, and I am happy to share them with you.

1. "A point of view can be a dangerous luxury when substituted for insight and understanding" (Marshall McLuhan). Advocacy puts you in a position of "stance." When you

advocate, you are trying to impart or enforce a particular action, position, or set of principles. You are trying to persuade by *arguing* for the position you are advocating.

2. "Wonder is the foundation of all philosophy, inquiry the progress, ignorance the end" (Michel de Montaigne). Inquiry is an attempt to *understand* the position of others rather than change their opinions. Once you consider and appreciate the opposing party's position, ask questions, practice active listening, think, and make them think.

3. "Reason and free inquiry are the only effectual agents against error" (Thomas Jefferson). When you have spent time to understand and validate others' perspective, ask questions that will make them think about *your* position. For example, "Do we know what this will look like from a budget standpoint? What do you think of the financials if we move forward?" Inquiry encourages contemplation. Contemplation helps you find clarity that will influence your audience.

This is not to say that advocacy is the root of all evil. There is a time and place for both approaches; however, advocacy can often interfere and short-circuit communication. Advocacy accounts for a lot of unnecessary conflict where both sides focus on convincing the other rather than understanding or compromising. Advocacy can breed contempt and doubt.

The next time you are compelled to advocate, pause. Ask questions that will help you understand the other side. Show them that you respect them and want to know more. After all you likely have a common goal for the result; it's just a matter of how you get there. Once you understand the alternate point of view, flip to questioning that will make your audience contemplate and consider yours and possibly *reconsider* theirs. With the right line of questioning, you will be poised to influence others to action.

Influence through Active Listening

Any married couple will tell you there is a difference between hearing and listening. Well, there is also a difference between listening and active listening. Hearing is just that—you hear the words someone else says. Listening is processing the words someone else says so you can understand them. Active listening is not only understanding but also inquiring into the words and the other person's thoughts to confirm your understanding. Keep in mind that not everyone clearly communicates exactly what they are thinking; to that end, active listening involves repeating what the person said back to them to confirm that you do, in fact, understand their perspective.

Influence through Clarity

Ever listened really closely to someone and at the end not really knew what they meant or what they wanted you to do? Sure, you have. Now have you listened to other people and no matter what topic they are chatting with you about, it is super clear what they mean? This is the difference between communicating with and without clarity. And guess what, the more complex the topic, the more important this is. Sometimes you are the expert who needs to talk about a subject matter that's new to your audience. If you don't communicate with clarity, you've wasted not only your time but also your audience's time.

If you

- establish a trusted *brand* that others can rely on,
- build and nurture *relationships*,
- *communicate* with clarity and consistency, and
- develop a high *emotional quotient*,
- your *influence* will grow exponentially. Wield it responsibly.

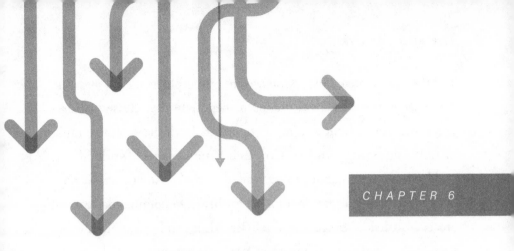

CHAPTER 6

Be Legendary

As a Fearless Leader, you have the opportunity to leave an exponential imprint on the world. Your imprint will be your legacy. And your legacy has the power to be *legendary*. Ask yourself this: What do I want my legacy to be? What lasting impact do I want to leave on the world? How can I be an inspirational *legend* to others?

It was September 1990 in my senior year of college, and I was thinking about the kind of company I wanted to work for upon graduation. I was beginning to narrow the field when I picked up the book *On Wings of Eagles: The Inspiring True Story of One Man's Patriotic Spirit—and His Heroic Mission to Save His Countrymen*. I'm not sure what surprised me more, reading a book voluntarily or the impact the book had on me.

It's the story of how two American businessmen were held hostage in Iran during the Middle East hostage crisis in 1978 and how one man took matters into his own hands; that man was H. Ross Perot. Perot was the CEO and founder of Electronic Data Systems (EDS), and the two captive businessmen were his employees, Paul and Bill. The U.S. government was unable to negotiate the release of Ross's employees, so he built a team of volunteers from the executive ranks of EDS and brought in Ret. Col. Bull Simons, famed World War II and Vietnam commando, to free the imprisoned Americans. Simons began organizing a plan that called for his EDS commando team to create a diversion, break into the Qasr Prison, and then grab the two men in the confusion. The rescue was a success, and Perot became a legend in that day.

When I finished the book, I knew EDS was the only company I wanted to work for upon graduation. I was disappointed but undeterred when I didn't get an interview with EDS when they visited our campus, but I still put my only white shirt, gray pants, and blue blazer on and waited for the EDS recruiter to check in, and then I jumped him with my résumé and all the reasons I needed to interview with him. He agreed to lunch, and three months later I was a Phase I at EDS, sitting in orientation in Plano, Texas. Within the very first hour of my professional career, we were talking core values with our president, Jeff Heller, and the importance of them as an EDS employee, and in that moment, I knew I was where I was meant to be.

Now you don't have to storm prisons fearlessly to be legendary, but I will share with you four pathways to building an exponential legacy of leadership.

First, *lead* others through a clear vision and the resources to achieve that vision—together.

Second, *coach* others to be the best versions of themselves. Take time every week to invest a little extra time to show someone how to improve a specific skill or attribute. Daily coaching is one of the easiest and best ways you can leave a lasting impact on the most amount of people. Thirty minutes of coaching may change the trajectory of someone's life.

Third, be a *mentor*. Slow down and take quality time to invest in those around you. Look around your circle of friends, family members, and colleagues and pick a person to take under your wing and send down the path of leadership. Chances are you owe a great deal of your success to the mentors in your life, both personally and professionally.

Fourth, *cultivate*. When you lead fearlessly by encouraging others to do good, to serve, and to be leaders, they, in turn, are motivated to encourage others to do good, to serve, and to be leaders. You exponentially remove the fear, uncertainty, and doubt that hold so many of us back from reaching our potential.

Finally, find ways to *give* with no expectation of receiving.

Lead

When you make the decision to *lead*, you build an exponential legacy of leadership. Let's try to quantify it. If you lead ten people who then lead another ten people who then lead another ten people to achieve a common goal, you will have impacted over one thousand lives on this planet.

What if I told you that simply by leading ten people, you will have removed instances of fear, uncertainty, and doubt half a million times over the next ten years? That's five hundred bouts of fear you assisted in crushing, five hundred flashes of uncertainty you helped beat, and five hundred moments of doubt you helped erase. Let's say that the average person deals with feelings of FUD several times a month. Multiply that by the thousand people you exponentially impacted, and you have over half a million opportunities to instill Fearless Leadership in others.

Now imagine instilling Fearless Leadership in one hundred people during your lifetime, and the number exponentially climbs to over *one billion* instances of empowering others to win the daily battle against their FUD. And when you wake up every day and make the decision to be a Fearless Leader, you will intentionally generate over one billion positive outcomes for people across the world. A legendary legacy of leadership.

Coach

Coaching can be highly effective. Now the purpose and process of coaching is different from leading, managing, or mentoring. Leading is all about taking responsibility to inspire and organize a team that is focused on achieving something the company and leader need accomplished versus something that might only benefit that team. Managing is all about tactically achieving that common goal that the company and leader are focused upon. It involves managing tasks, projects, people, and yourself. Mentoring plays a much broader role of cultivating an individual's career and overall personal and professional development.

Coaching, similar to mentoring, is focused on an individual. The difference is that coaching drives at a specific goal through learning. For example, coaching someone to make a sales call, to perform a job function better, or to complete a twenty-yard pass. Coaching requires patience, intention, and pace.

When you make the decision to *coach*, you will immediately see the impact you have on others. If leading and mentoring is the long game, then coaching is the short game. Think of coaching as leadership and mentorship in a bite-size daily serving. So how can you serve up bite-size coaching every day? Follow these three simple steps:

- *Slow Down:* In today's world this can be tough. You've got fifty new emails in your inbox, an endless action list, and six back-to-back meetings, but you still need to make the decision to slow down to help someone else—to invest in someone else's success.

- *Invest Time:* As you scan your fifty emails and come across one from a colleague or a mentee who is struggling, instead of replying in a thirty-second email, get up from your desk or pick up the phone and coach the person, real-time, bite-size coaching that lasts five to ten minutes.

- *Coach Up:* You've slowed down and made time to help someone; the next step is to coach the person up, not down. You intuitively know what I mean, but sometimes we don't slow down enough or make enough time, and our coaching can come off unintentionally as managing. Coaching comes from a place of empathy; use your teaching voice, explain, show, and demonstrate. Listen and learn; don't tell and dictate. Coaching in bite-size increments always leaves the player feeling better for your support.

By now you know that there is no way I can talk about coaches in this "Be Legendary" chapter without revisiting Bill Belichick. Belichick is a coaching legend because he built a simple system that sustained twenty years of success of near-dynasty proportion in a sport that's constructed to not allow dynasties to exist. Professional football has a salary cap, which means a team can't keep all of their own draft picks because they can't afford to, which also means one team can't grab all the top players.

What also makes Belichick's coaching style successful is his willingness to be flexible with the system while continuing to bring in players who fit his system and who can be successful in his system regardless of experience. On one of his weekly interviews on WEEI's *The Greg Hill Show*, Belichick stated, "A player's experience can be irrelevant in comparison to their ability to simply learn a new system." Wait, what?

He went on to say, "I think when you coach a team or when you coach a player, you just don't sit there and think about, is he a rookie, or is he a second-year player? Is he a seventh-year player, or is he a ninth-year player? You just coach him to try and help him get better, and that's a sliding scale. You just have to find that balance with each player regardless of what year he's in or what position he plays. That's just coaching."[14] I couldn't have said it better.

Mentor

Let's break down what a mentor is. First, they are volunteers. Yes, even in companies that have formally structured mentoring programs, the mentor does not receive any compensation for the role. Second, a mentor is focused purely on the development of their mentee and helping them achieve their career goals—not their own. Third, mentors volunteer their time to advance the careers of their mentees with no personal or professional benefit expected in return.

Given that *mentoring* is volunteering to develop individuals to achieve their career goals and advancement with nothing expected in return, it makes what the six mentors—Vicki, Val, Bill, John, Gary B., and Gary F., who changed my life—did for me even more special.

---

14   Hayden Bird, "Bill Belichick on his coaching philosophy, Kendrick Bourne's energy, and the 'Bills Mafia," Boston.com, November 29, 2021, https://www.boston.com/?post_type=post&p=23765526.

All the sessions we spent together, all the advice they gave me, all the foolish decisions they stopped me from making, and all the ways they encouraged me were just that—for me! All six of these people were always incredibly busy, but somehow they made time to sit with me and patiently teach me. They taught me both business and personal lessons—from which job opportunity to take to picking out wine in a restaurant so that I did not embarrass myself.

Great mentors fulfill several responsibilities over the course of their mentorship with their mentee. This is something I have broken down into six roles.

Role Model

Role model is perhaps the foundation for what makes a mentee select a mentor. Personally, all of my mentors were role models inside and outside of the office. And when I stop to think about it, they've never stopped being my role models. I modeled their positive behaviors and actions that I witnessed at the office. But I also molded myself in how they conducted themselves in their personal lives and in the community. I took note of how they ran meetings, how they cared for their employees, and the leadership roles they took in serving others.

Performer

Performer comes on the heels of being a role model. Oftentimes, we get a chance to see our mentor in the workplace. How we see them act and the results they achieve become appealing to us as mentees. So to be a great mentor, you have to continually be a high performer. More simply stated, great mentors keep setting the bar for what a great leader means day in and day out.

When I first went out to Silicon Valley, I was an unsophisticated thirty-year-old. Gary B. was the CEO of the company who just hired me, and I was second in command. While I did gain a ton of business acumen from Gary over the years, I also learned about culture and how to be an executive.

I remember that one of his shared wisdoms was "Brendan, just remember, when you're at an event, you're working. Your job is to make every single person there feel special." I still embrace that wisdom today. Gary mentored me in and out of the office, and I remember one evening at our favorite restaurant in Menlo Park, California. Gary B. and I sat and discussed wine over dinner. He was a wine enthusiast and always ordered for all, no matter who was dining. I thought that was a pretty cool skill to learn and one I wanted to emulate. The previous weekend, I had gone to a wine store to gain more insight, and I even walked away with a little cheat sheet to keep in my wallet. But what they couldn't teach me was what wine to order with whom and at what price point, which Gary B. had an aptitude for. Well, all I can say is thank you to Gary B.—you taught me well!

Teacher

Teacher is the cornerstone role of a great mentorship. Great mentors are able to patiently teach their mentees how to achieve their desired goals. They are able to facilitate the transfer of their competency, knowledge, and wisdom. Oftentimes they are required to do this by being adaptable to their mentee while still being able to challenge their student. Being a great teacher is not easy. It takes patience, practice, and a sincere willingness to do it.

Advocate

Advocate is the selfless role of representing others and advancing their cause. Sometimes great mentors educate and inform others of their mentees' skills and their experience—they *put the mentee on the radar.* Other times the mentor is even more assertive and may launch a passionate campaign for their mentee to be recognized, transferred, and/or promoted. I'm fortunate to have had such mentors.

In June of 1997, two of my mentors, Val and Bill, called me into their office and notified me that I had just been promoted to a new role at corporate in Plano, Texas. At twenty-seven years old, I was all about promotions, so I was excited and took off two days later for my new, better, cooler job without looking back. Years later when I became a mentor myself, I realized the depth of what Val and Bill had done for me. Though they were levels above me, I worked in the same business unit as Val and Bill, and I was doing a decent job. That meant my transfer was a loss for their division. Even so, they selflessly advocated for me, put my name in the ring for a promotion, and were excited for me when I received it. They had weakened their own team to promote my career and personal development. When I reflect on this, I am ever more grateful for the power of their advocacy, encouragement, and counsel that they chose to bestow on me.

Communicator

Communicator is the role that makes the day-to-day mentorship work well. Great mentors are great listeners. They listen actively, know when to step in and say something, and know how to say it. They listen between the lines and have an ability to see the big picture for their mentees—even when their mentees can't see it for themselves. Oftentimes they connect the dots of a problem, a challenge, or an opportunity for their mentee based on having greater business and life experience.

Some of the best mentors take an inquiry approach and simply ask their mentees a number of questions that cause them to reflect more deeply, think more broadly, and slow down before making any quick decisions. I know a few times when my mentors were being extremely tactful in asking me some questions that I really knew the answers to but probably didn't want to admit in the moment. In that respect their diplomacy kept me in check and did so without bruising my ego by letting me arrive at my own decision.

Gary F. was one of those mentors who knew how to connect the dots for me. One time I asked Gary to meet with me so I could talk to him about a job I applied for and didn't get. As soon as we sat down, I started right in, telling him how crazy it was that they chose the other guy over me. He was less qualified than I was. I was better than him and so on.

Gary just looked at me and said, "I agree. I absolutely would've picked you over him, and everything you've said is true, but why do you want that job? It's a dead-end job."

"What do you mean?" I asked. "It's a promotion."

"Yes, a promotion into a dead industry. That industry grows at 2 percent a year. Wait for a better opportunity."

At that time I didn't see the big picture. I just saw a lost promotion, and I didn't like to lose. A year later a better opportunity did come along. And when I saw Gary after landing that job, he said, "Just imagine, if you had gotten that other job, you wouldn't have even been a candidate for this position." I'm forever grateful for Gary's patience and wisdom.

Advisor

Advisor is the apex role of the mentor-mentee relationship. As the mentor develops, advances, and grows their mentee, there are times when they advise their mentee on decisions that make a difference. Mentors have the ability to see the bigger picture, have a 360-degree perspective, and have the experience of "having been there and done that."

In 2001 I had completed my first CEO role and was sitting on the sidelines, honoring a noncompete. I flew to New York City to meet with John, a longtime mentor and CEO of a large company, to ask him for his advice on what I should do next. As I was sitting out the noncompete, I was also doing some consulting to keep myself busy. During my meeting with John, we both determined I could help him, his company, and the board of directors with a small consulting engagement.

After leading the engagement for about two weeks, John and I realized the synergy we had with one another and the good work we were accomplishing for his company. Over an evening drink by Central Park, John and I worked out a new role in his company that was clear of any noncompete and brought great value to his company. What started as a simple mentoring session had turned into a wonderful job offer. I am sincerely grateful for John's advice and unique perspective.

Mentoring is not a solo sport. It takes two to be successful, which means mentees have their roles and responsibilities to fulfill in this partnership. I've categorized the four mentee roles below.

1. *Worker:* This is where the mentorship can start and accelerate or start and stop. Remember, mentors are acting on a volunteer basis and are investing their own time willingly

with nothing expected in return. Well, maybe they do expect a few things in return. At the top of the list is the expectation that their mentee is working hard in their job. No one is suggesting perfection, but we are certainly talking about performing at your best. It is understood that, from time to time, a mentee's job performance may make a misstep, and that is when the mentor can really step in and add value for the mentee. It is vital that your mentor knows through your actions that you are committed to your career and personal growth.

2. *Student:* This is the core element required for a great mentorship. Productive mentees seek to absorb as much as possible from their mentors. Business lessons, life lessons, best practices, common mistakes—they are emulating these. Being a student requires an ability to learn and a willingness to change. Being a great student in the classroom is not all that different from being a great student in your profession. You may not necessarily sit at a desk when the bell rings or watch your mentor at a blackboard; however, our professional world is still a classroom. Being a productive mentee is about being prepared for your next lesson, seeking new ideas with the focus on improving yourself and holding yourself accountable.

3. *Communicator:* This is what makes the mentorship successful. It is the responsibility of the mentee to articulate where they want to go, who they want to be, and what they want to accomplish. The mentee's vision may be a bit foggy, and it is the mentor's role to help clear that fog. At the end of the day, the mentee must be able to communicate their needs, challenges, and opportunities. Lastly, it is

very important that mentees are able to receive constructive feedback and be coachable. To get better and grow, we must get uncomfortable.

4. *Doer:* This is what determines the return on investment for the overall mentorship. Through the six roles of a mentor and the first three roles of a mentee, we have set the groundwork for what matters most—the mentee incorporating all the wisdom and knowledge shared by their mentor into action. Successful mentees GSD and keep their mentor apprised of their progress.

Creating a Mentorship Program to Change Your Life

If you are ready to invest in your own career and accelerate your development, I encourage you to find a mentor and begin the journey. I have participated in both formal and informal mentor programs, and they have produced tremendous results.

Depending on where you work, you may or may not have a formal mentor program available to you. If you do, great. Find out how it works and get started. If your company does not have a formal program, then look around and make a list of five people you view as a role model and to whom you have some type of access. While it is important that you have access to these individuals, it is not important that you have a preestablished relationship. Once you are committed to being a successful mentee, start at the top of the list and reach out to the first person and ask them if they would be willing to mentor you over the coming year.

I believe those of us who have been mentored and have the opportunity to mentor others have a social responsibility to do so. Trust me, it will be worth your time and effort. It's wonderful to have someone ask you to help them navigate their success no matter where you are in your leadership journey. In fact, I still seek out mentors for my own personal and professional growth because I know I still have so much to learn. The world is full of tremendous wisdom; you just have to reach out and absorb it.

Cultivate

To *cultivate* means "to foster the growth of," "to further," or "to encourage." Fearless Leaders choose to practice these actions with everyone who touches their lives. The level of cultivation varies from situation to situation, group to group, and individual to individual. Some will find encouragement through your positive reputation or your brand without ever meeting you in person. For others it may be the time and effort you have made to connect with them, to listen to them, and to know them that builds their courage. And there are those in your smaller circle whom you are more purposeful in your cultivation through deep relationships and individualized coaching and mentoring.

Leaders have clear and present opportunities each day in every interaction to inspire leadership at work and in the communities in which they live—our neighbors, our kids, our social circles, our places of faith, our gyms, and our coffee houses—and really anyone we meet is an opportunity to begin to light the fuse of leadership for another person. So many people in life have never been told they, too, can be a leader, let alone have another person invest in them.

Leaders cultivate in a variety of ways, and I'm going to share with you four leaders who excel at fostering growth, furthering, and encouraging others. Two of the leaders are from my own community;

one is a former colleague, but I'll start with the one we all know, Martin Luther King Jr.

I don't think there has ever been anyone in our history who has united masses of individuals with a single message as successfully as Dr. King. Church by church, gathering by gathering, politician by politician, and citizen by citizen, Dr. King communicated his message and inspired the masses to not only follow but also help him lead the cause. Dr. King was the driving force behind the Montgomery bus boycott and the 1963 March on Washington that led to the passage of the Civil Rights Act and the Voting Rights Act, an explosive time in history in which Dr. King led not with brute force but by listening, communicating, relating, and cultivating a corps of leaders with an empowering and uplifting belief in his message of equality for all. Now there may not be another leader equal to Dr. King in my lifetime, but there are individuals all around us who, on a smaller scale, cultivate those around them for the greater good.

Judge Joseph N. Laplante is the definition of "give more than you get." I have watched him in action too many times to count, and what I have come to realize is he is not only truly skilled at giving but he's also highly skilled at helping others give, and to me that's the ultimate example of encouraging others for the greater good. Over the years he has volunteered for a range of organizations including the Police Athletic League and the Boys and Girls Clubs, but what makes Joe stand out is that he goes beyond those roles to draw in the greater community through his extensive network.

I know I am only one of many who get the occasional texts from Joe saying, "Hey, I know you are going to XYZ. Do you think you could give this person a ride?" or "Hey, do you think you could spare a couple of hours next Saturday to help me with a project?" You say yes, and on that Saturday, you find yourself meeting up with ten, twenty, or however many people of varying skills Joe has assembled for the task at hand. Setting up a basketball court or serving a fundraising dinner, it doesn't matter. When Joe asks, you show up. And you show up because everything Joe does is for the betterment of our community. He has taken his extensive professional and personal network to cultivate a community of givers.

Aaron Quinn, the athletic director at Middlebury College, continues to cultivate a positive influence in his student athletes. Aaron's gift is his authenticity and his ability to always be present with the people he's with. Even though he had staff to take care of basic tasks, I have seen him at events being the one to make sure every student athlete had enough pizza or when realizing folks were out of water, running down the hall to get more. He's always the guy who will pop his head in to check that everyone's good and if they need anything before he heads out. Aaron is the kind of guy who makes everyone believe that they matter. He's not about his title; he's about helping the kids, and I guarantee that there isn't a student athlete who's attended Middlebury College who doesn't feel the presence and the positive influence Aaron Quinn has cultivated.

Five Ways Companies Can Cultivate a Positive Work Environment

I recently read a statistic that made me think about how many companies struggle with employee satisfaction and workplace cultures. According to a *Wall Street Journal* article, 51 percent of American workers reported being satisfied with their jobs. This number was touted as being the highest since 2005, an indicator of "rising job contentment."[15] It was a cause for celebration. How can the dissatisfaction of 49 percent of our workforce be something to celebrate?

Companies simply cannot afford to accept 51 percent as an acceptable employee satisfaction rate, nor should they. It is well known that increased employee happiness results in increased productivity and profitability. When employees are connected to their company's strategic direction and can see how their goals contribute to that vision, their job satisfaction increases. And it is only with engaged employees that companies can deliver better solutions and service for their clients.

Creating strong employee engagement and connection to the company starts by building an easily understood and supported culture. Here are five ways to get there.

1. Define your culture: Whether or not you set it, your culture will define itself. The question is, did you unconsciously or consciously define it? If you discover your culture has been more unconscious than deliberate, take it as an opportunity to review your culture in depth. Start by identifying core values that make your company great and the attributes that have developed over time that need to be amplified. Then articulate those values in a way that all employees can understand and rally around. It is important to distill your culture into something that can be easily described by anyone who works for you so your employees are as equipped as possible to be brand ambassadors and advocates.

2. Hire to your culture: If you have defined your culture as collaborative, high integrity, service oriented, and innovative,

---

15   Lauren Weber, "US Workers Report Highest Job Satisfaction Since 2005," The Wall Street Journal, August 29, 2018, https://www.wsj.com/articles/u-s-workers-report-highest-job-satisfaction-since-2005-1535544000.

as you look at candidates, you should be asking, "Is this a collaborative, innovative, service-oriented person who has integrity?" Whatever your culture is, you need to be hiring the right employees for that culture.

3. Make sure your culture is part of the performance management process: Are you measuring and reinforcing the attributes of your culture? If you say collaboration is important to your culture but it's not discussed in a performance review, then you're sending the message it's not important.

4. Promote the right attributes of culture: Part of building and sustaining a company culture is looking ahead to identify who on your team can carry that culture forward as leaders. If you say your culture is hardworking, innovative, and collaborative, then that's what your leaders must reflect.

5. Address the employees who are misaligned with the company's culture: It's tough to build a culture, but it just takes a few people to dismantle it. Organizations often find this hard to do, but sometimes it's as simple as having a difficult conversation with that team member. When someone is struggling in their role, they often can see that they have challenges, and more often than not, they are aware of their own misalignment to the culture. Sometimes just having this difficult conversation brings awareness to the individual that they should look for a different position (whether that is inside the company or elsewhere) or take active steps to improve their performance and resolve the situation.

Proactively building a healthy company culture can be challenging, but it is the primary way companies can move the needle not just on employee engagement and satisfaction but on client retention and satisfaction as well. Defining your culture, then using it as your guidepost for hiring, performance management, and promotion can lead to significant gains in productivity and profitability. As each company takes action, we gradually begin to shift the workplace culture so that a 51 percent satisfaction is no longer a success; rather, it is just a starting point to make our work lives better. Don't settle for 51 percent. Set the bar much higher for your team's satisfaction and then work hard each year to beat the previous year.

Build It and They Will Come

John Geraci, managing partner at LGA, is a great example of the intentional and authentic development of a culture that puts its people first. In an industry that hails billable hours and seventy-plus-hour workweeks as crowns of success, John dared to flip the narrative and create a work culture inspired by the movie *Field of Dreams.*

> When I first started in the industry, you were expected to do whatever one of the bosses asked you to do. It was understood that work was your number one commitment, and your family was second. During tax season the owner would always come around on Fridays and say, "Can you come in tomorrow and do 1040s? We'd really love to have you help us catch up." I always said yes.
>
> Sometimes on those Saturdays, he'd come around and ask the same question, "Can you come in tomorrow?" One of those "tomorrows" was my wife's birthday, so on that Saturday when he asked, "John, can you help us out tomorrow?" I said, "I can't because it's Wendy's birthday, and I'm spending the day with her. We're going to go out to dinner and everything."

Without missing a beat, he said, "Why don't you have her come in tomorrow night? We're having dinner cooked here on Sunday, and we'll do a cake for her." We just weren't given a no option, so I had to go home that night and tell my wife that I had committed her to coming into the firm for her birthday. That's just how it was. Today I wouldn't think about asking someone to come in if it was their wife's birthday; I would respect that.

It's funny to think about it now because back then the partner's response was considered nice. A more common response in the industry was, "I don't care whose birthday it is. You're working tomorrow." It was considered a badge of honor to be the one who worked the most hours in any given week during tax season.

I grew up at VCC, where I had the opportunity to witness visionary leadership that led to explosive growth during my tenure there. But in 2009 after being with the company for twelve years, I knew it was time for me to move on, and I found my way to LGA.

In his new position, John envisioned a work environment that put people first. One of the initial steps on the path to that vision was creating opportunities and transparency for LGA's employees around their own career growth.

I would meet with all the new employee prospects, and I would always describe our firm as a ball of clay. And I'd say, "Look, if you want to have your fingerprints all over something that you can look back on and to be proud of what you were able to help build, this is the place for you because we care about you. We care about what you think. We always want you to feel like it's your firm, not our firm." It was exciting to start shifting the culture in that way, but I didn't fully realize the scope of what we needed to do until I attended a *Boston Business Journal* Best Places to Work event, which had former winners as the panelists.

As the panelists shared what worked for them and why their organizations were the best places to work, one of the things that stood out to me was the level of connectivity with the entire team, starting with the transparency of the firm's leadership. At the time, I was the youngest partner in our firm, but I was also the top contender to be the next managing partner. When I walked away from that event, I came to realize how carefully I was leading for fear of being perceived as too out there. I wasn't being true to myself and who I was as a leader, and in that moment, I knew I had to start leading with complete authenticity.

I cared about our teams. I cared about our people. It was time I got to really know them. I wanted to get to know them. As I continued to move into the managing partner role, I was less involved in direct client service, which meant I had less opportunity to be influential across a wider group of people organically. Instead, I was going to have to find ways to connect and engage. I created opportunities to meet with every team member within the first sixty days of their start so that we'd have a chance to get to know each other on a more personal level. That helped create more connectivity to the team as we were growing and to give everybody a chance to understand my tone, tenor, and vision and to ask me any question that they had.

John eventually led the partners to understand that they had to care about their teams more than they cared about themselves, a hard concept to embrace in an industry where people work so hard to be a partner that they think once they get there, everybody owes them something.

I had to get them to understand that servant leadership is really what this generation is going to need if we're going to thrive as an organization and that the "leaders eat last" concept had to apply to us. We can't wait for our people to do X, and then we respond with Y. It doesn't work like that.

John was brazen enough to push back on the industry's entrenched perspective that clients are number one at all costs. His vision was to make LGA's team members number one.

If we give people a great organization that they really believe in, when we ask them to run through walls alongside us, that will feel a whole lot different from just expecting them to do it without receiving anything from us first.

Reality and John's vision of a *Field of Dreams*—"build it, and they will come" work culture—are now in alignment. In 2019 LGA was voted as BBJ Best Place to Work.

> Our leadership team were thrilled to be named as a Best Place to Work honoree, but for me it wasn't about the recognition of being voted as best place to work. It was more about a bit of validation that all the effort we put into creating a special organization where people truly felt like they counted and that they were the most important part of our company was working. But there is more work to be done. Leading an organization is a marathon, not a sprint. No matter what you seem to achieve or accomplish along the way, there will always be other areas that must continually be worked on. I congratulated our team when BBJ named us an honoree, and then I told them, "This is just the beginning. There's no pause button when you're building a great environment for your team."

Give

Leading means giving—giving time, direction, support, encouragement, wisdom so that common goals and visions can be achieved. Fearless Leaders also engage in philanthropy, whether that is through time, money, or both. I was fortunate to grow up with parents and a sister who gave endlessly. My mom was a volunteer art teacher at an elementary school, a team mom to almost every team I was on, a Cub Scout leader for my brothers, a eucharistic minister at our church, and a tireless activist on many fronts for kids with special needs. Every step of the way, my dad was next to her, fundraising or serving as treasurer.

My sister freely gave the gift of making everyone feel special. One of the ways she did that was by standing outside the locker room before every football game and again at halftime to encourage every player who came out with a high five and a "Come on, Corey. Come on, Joe. Come on … you guys got this." Every player at every game. Her unconditional love and giving to others inspired our whole community.

As a kid my weekends were filled with volunteer activities; I just didn't know I was volunteering. I never thought of it as a special role; it was simply what you do for others and for your community. I am so thankful that my family imprinted the legacy of giving on me.

Giving is so easy, incredibly rewarding, and beneficial to our bodies and minds.

Mayo Clinic's article "The Art of Kindness" outlines the benefits to our body when we participate in acts of kindness. Kindness has been shown to

- increase self-esteem, empathy, and compassion;
- decrease stress levels by lowering our blood pressure and the stress hormone cortisol; and
- improve low moods and enhance relationships through connectivity to others.

But there's more. Acting with kindness can physiologically positively change your brain through the boosting of neurotransmitters in the brain, serotonin and dopamine, that increase our feelings of satisfaction and well-being and endorphins, which are our body's natural painkillers.[16]

We all have the opportunity to give in more ways every day and to do it with no expectation of getting anything in return—to run a 5K race for a cause, to buy Girl Scout cookies, to serve meals at a local shelter, to be a Big Sister at your local Police Athletic League, to coach a youth sports team, to donate blood, or to support any cause that fuels your body, mind, and soul with goodness. The opportunities are endless.

---

16   Steve Siegle, "The art of kindness," Mayo Clinic Health System, May 29, 2020, https://www.mayoclinichealthsystem.org/hometown-health/speaking-of-health/the-art-of-kindness#:~:text=Good%20for%20the%20body,be%20healthier%20and%20live%20longer.

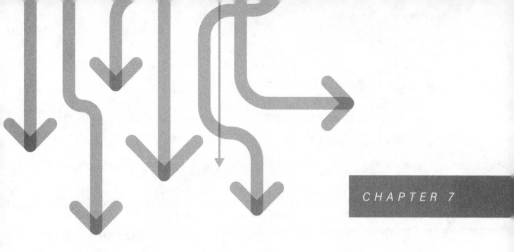

CHAPTER 7

Begin

We've looked at a wide range of attributes and practices that support and nurture Fearless Leaders. Now it's time to start bundling those attributes and practices together and see how they can work in harmony to transform our leadership intentions and our lives.

This chapter leads us on a discovery of how emerging leaders make plans and *launch* careers, how practicing leaders and individual contributors who feel stuck can make the *leap* into a new paradigm, how Fearless Leaders *overcome* and triumph in the face of crisis, and how each of us can build our lives and leadership approaches around a practice that consistently pushes us to *grow*.

A leader can best prepare to *launch*, *leap*, *overcome*, and *grow* by first hitting the pause button and taking the time to *recognize* the skills they have developed, the growth they have already achieved, and the leadership opportunities that are already present. Pausing to recognize also helps you identify the leadership skills and attributes that you will need to develop to get you where your vision is leading you.

Recognize

Whenever I give someone a promotion, the first thing they say is, "Thanks for the promotion."

And I always respond, "I didn't give you the promotion. You gave yourself the promotion. My job was strictly recognizing that your performance is at a director level." Or maybe it's a manager level or a VP level, whatever the level of promotion. The truth is they promoted themselves by demonstrating the skills and their readiness for more responsibility. My job as their leader was to recognize that in them, even if they didn't see it in themselves. Your job as a leader is to recognize the abilities, strengths, and growth in those you are leading.

Mentors and coaches can be pivotal in recognizing the growth we might not see in ourselves. They're on the outside looking in, providing them a different and more objective perspective. Don't be shy about checking in with them and asking, "What do you see as my greatest areas of growth over the past six months, year, five years?" It's not just about "How can I improve and grow as a leader?" It's also about "How *have* I improved and grown as a leader?"

Maybe you don't see yourself as a leader yet or are just not ready for the next leadership level, but if you take the time to sit back and review where you were a year or two ago versus where you are now, you'll have the opportunity to see your personal growth and how that has impacted your professional skills, attributes, and opportunities. You may realize that what you are accomplishing today may not have been possible a year ago because you lacked the abilities, and now through your own personal and professional growth, you're able to achieve. Don't forget to pay attention to how you're leading too. Recognize what skills you are using to lead and how you can leverage those skills to lead better.

When at First You Recognize

There is no one more self-aware and intentional about her own development as a leader than Amanda Rogers. I was introduced to Amanda at a high school sports awards dinner. We spoke briefly, and a couple of days later, I received an email from her telling me that she had seen my LinkedIn profile and was impressed with the work I was doing and wanted to learn more. I invited her to come to the office for a meeting. At just twenty-three, Amanda, like Kirsten Rhodes, oozed natural leadership attributes with her positive energy, humility, confidence, and willingness to learn. I didn't have a job opening for her at the time, but I offered her a contractor position at ten hours per week. She accepted, and immediately, this emerging leader's willingness to collaborate and step up to new challenges was evident.

Fast-forward ten years, and Amanda is a vice president on the senior leadership team at a $2 billion company. What really stands out with Amanda is not only her willingness to continually stretch herself in new ways but also her ability to recognize her strengths and abilities and how to best leverage them for the betterment of those around her.

> If you were to ask me about the early stages of becoming a leader, I would say that from an early age, I was willing to take initiative in some way in different situations. This was probably a function of playing sports, where my teammates and I were taught to take initiative, and I quickly adopted those principles in other places like school, organizations I was part of, and ultimately my work. I enjoyed leading but mostly because I could see that I could help my teammates and others by setting a vision and supporting them in getting there—however big or small that vision was. I didn't know it at the time,

> but I started to see in college and can definitely see
> now how that laid the foundation for the leader I have
> become—setting a vision, communicating that vision,
> and supporting a group of people to achieve it.

Amanda recalls a time in college when she was a member of a group of six students working on an organizational behavior project during her undergraduate studies. At the end of the project, the group provided each other written feedback. There was this one student on the team who was from China and struggled with her English. The peer feedback she provided Amanda was that Amanda always made her feel so welcomed and part of the team and that she appreciated the opportunity to really feel heard.

> I hadn't thought of it during the project, but that
> feedback made me reflect on my role in the group, and
> I realized that I had gone out of my way to help her
> feel comfortable. That's when it really struck me that I
> had the starting point of emotional intelligence. While I
> recognized it as an ability, I don't think I labeled it EQ at
> the time, but now fifteen or so years later, I consciously
> leverage that skill to positively influence those around
> me.

That college peer feedback was the conscious start of Amanda's leadership journey, a start that stemmed from Amanda's desire to make an impact on others, especially those who may not have the confidence to do it themselves yet. One way Amanda fulfills this desire is by finding opportunities to fulfill the dreams of her team.

I make a concerted effort to really listen and understand what the dreams and visons of each of my team
members are. I store them in a mental file and try to
identify opportunities as they come up. Not too long
ago, I had a woman on my team who had expressed
interest in becoming a manager. When we identified a
new role that was intended to be a direct report to me, I
saw a natural fit for her to lead that team member—she
had shown that she could do it. It worked for everyone.
In that moment I was able to help her achieve one of
her goals.

That level of listening and understanding can be done in a group
setting as well. Amanda has developed the skill to feel the energy of
a group, to discern each participant's level of engagement, and to
adjust how she's leading and interacting to keep everyone engaged.
This includes awareness of the varying levels of understanding of each
participant.

I feel that I can tell if someone is further along on the
material we are covering and ready to move on. Then
I can see that others might not yet be ready. In those
cases I try to bring the person who is ready into the
conversation as a sort of cofacilitator. "Hey, Joe, you've
done this before. Can you share what happened and
how you solved it?" It's pretty simple. I have seen other
leaders do it, but it requires the ability to really pay
attention to where each individual is at.

Amanda's recognition of her EQ strength and her ability to
influence others combined with her willingness to seek out help

from mentors when needed have enabled her to not only successfully launch her career but also make significant career leaps.

Leadership and Its Inherent Power

It's important to recognize our own abilities and growth and the abilities and growth of those we lead. It's critical that leaders also recognize their responsibilities and inherent power of their role as leader.

Leading doesn't only happen when you are a CEO; it doesn't even always happen intentionally. If others, even one person, are influenced by you, you are leading. Parents lead their children, older siblings lead their younger siblings—even when they don't want to—teachers lead their students, and sometimes they find themselves leading the parents of their students. Committed team members, whether on our sales team or bowling team, influence us to be better. How we influence isn't always positive. Leaders who don't appreciate or encourage can influence us to wonder what the point is and give ourselves permission to do less and to be less than our potential. Leading doesn't require a title or even conscious intention, but it always—always—requires responsibility for and recognition of its power.

I learned this the hard way during my second time as a CEO. In every company I work in, I frequently walk the building and talk to everybody. In this instance I chatted about conferences with one of the marketing staff and asked if they thought we should be out there, participating in conferences more. There was no directive on my part, just a casual "What do you think about … ?" kind of conversation. I didn't give it another thought, until I realized that the marketing department had been shut down for two days researching every conference in North America. I still vividly remember closing my office door and thinking, "That's flattering, but wow, I need to change how I approach people." Even when I wasn't trying to lead, they were trying to follow. That's powerful stuff.

Launch

We can't talk about launching your career without revisiting what your values, your vision, and your goals are. So if you didn't really dig into the content of chapter 3, "Be Good," and chapter 4, "Be Impactful," I suggest you go back before you try to move forward. Without having a clear understanding of those leadership attributes, it would be like deciding to bake "something." You don't know what you want to bake, so you throw a bunch of stuff in a bowl, mix it up, pop it in the oven, and hope for the best. Launching your career or any significant life change doesn't succeed by crossing your fingers and hoping for the best. Recognizing what you want and where you want to go, identifying the steps to get you there, and taking action on those steps do.

I encourage people, once they've established their goals, to add something bold. Say, your goal is to become a manager or director; whatever leadership level you're working toward, add something extra to that goal. What does that look like? Maybe it means I want to be a director, *and* I want to learn how to do it in at least two industries. Or I want to be a VP in my industry, *and* I want to do it in the States and in Europe. Bold can be scary, but it doesn't mean bold has to be your next step. In most cases it's not. Maybe that bold step is five years away or maybe even ten, but it's what keeps you stretching. When you don't include a *stretch* component, when you choose to play it safe, you can't lead fearlessly.

Sometimes that bold step can feel like a step backward, but if you're looking at the long game of attaining your vision, you have to assess the next steps based on the big picture. A salesperson who worked at HP Enterprise is a great example. Mike was twenty-eight or twenty-nine when he asked me to mentor him. At the time, he was making a ton of money as a successful salesperson, but he knew he wanted to grow into a leadership position. He told me he wanted my career. Mike was clear on his progression. He wanted to become a manager, then VP of sales, and after that he'd be CEO. I told him that was great and asked him what he was going to do when his first sales manager opportunity was offered to him. He said he was going to take it. Then I had to brace him for reality.

I said, "You're making $X now, and the sales manager position is going to offer you $X, -20 percent. What are you going to do then?"

Mike looked confused. "Whoa, why would I make less?"

"Because that's what entry-level sales managers make."

"But why would I take a step back?" he asked.

"Because your goals and vision are leading you down a different path."

Mike really wrestled with this concept, and we met a few more times to talk it through. I opened his eyes to the fact that sales managers make less than their top salespeople, and he just kept saying, "That's just wrong." I told him that it's how the world works, that the more his salespeople made, the more he would make but that his income would never be the same as the top salesperson.

"Why would anyone do that?" he asked.

These are the moments in life that we need to focus on the big picture, and so I broke it down for him that being a sales manager would lead him to a VP of sales position—which was one of his goals. At this level he'd be making $X again and 20 percent more, *plus* he would start to receive stock options in equity. While the *plus* stuff won't create W-2 income, I assured him it would create wealth income. If his goal was to maximize his W-2 over the next twenty years, I encouraged him to remain a top salesperson, but if he was playing the long game and he wanted to be CEO and maximize his wealth over the life of his career, then he was going to have to first take a step back. I asked Mike one final time, "What's your long game?"

"I want to run a company."

"Then I guess you have made your decision." In the end he decided to stick with his long game, and he's had tremendous success because he was willing to make less income for a number of years to take a big step forward.

What Got You Halfway up the Mountain May Not Get You to the Top

Meet Amy, a seasoned executive who was on the brink of becoming managing partner for a large consulting firm. She and the retiring managing partner had very different styles. The older managing partner led with a modest growth mindset; Amy was a "let's take the hill" kind of leader. There were six partners in all, and I was brought in to help all the partners with the transition. After my introductory kickoff meeting with all the partners, Amy came up to me and said, "Super glad you're here. You come highly recommended. Loved your kickoff talk. Good luck with the team. I don't really need to be part of this."

I smiled and said, "Amy, you're a hundred percent right. If you want to be one of the six partners, you don't need me at all. But if you want to become managing partner, you need me more than anybody else in the firm."

"Excuse me?" Amy asked.

"Right there," I said. "You're a little irritated right now."

"Yeah, you could say that."

"Well, managing partners don't get irritated over simple comments like that. You know, Amy, you are absolutely the alpha partner, and I can tell you that everybody in the room wants you to be the managing partner. They also all want to be the managing partner themselves, but they all know you're the right choice. They really do. I can also tell that if you don't change some of who you are as a leader, it will be impossible for you to manage the partners because they won't want to follow you."

"Hmm," was her response.

Amy is supersmart, and she could paint an incredible vision of where she wanted the firm to go, but her attitude with partners who may not be up to her speed was, "What's your problem?" and those people would be left behind. My job was to help Amy recognize that she needed to adjust her leadership to one that brought people along on her vision and how she was going to do that. If Amy was running one hundred miles per hour and another partner was running at sixty miles an hour, she was going to have to go shoulder to shoulder with them and teach them to run at seventy miles an hour, then eighty, helping them reach the highest speed they were capable of. Amy did an incredible job at slowing down and being a more patient leader. There were times she would share a situation she was having and ask, "What do I do with this person?" I would tell her to do nothing because that was how that person operates, and that wasn't going to change.

"But it irritates me," would be her inevitable response.

"Yup," I'd say and then ask, "How good of a partner are they?"

"Technically, they do a great job."

From there we would walk through a pros and cons list, and I would remind Amy that she was not there to "fix" everyone; she was there to make sure everyone was working toward the common goals and vision the firm was aspiring to. The fact was that what had worked for Amy to get to the level of partner just wasn't going to be enough to get her to the role of managing partner and be successful at it. By embracing the changes she needed to make, Amy was able to launch her successful managing partner career. Sometimes what has made you successful getting up the first half of the mountain isn't going to be what gets you to the top of the mountain. At different moments in our career, we reassess, adapt, and prepare for our next launch. Amy made her adjustments, and her firm continues every year to outpace the industry and beat their growth plans, a true success story of slowing down to go faster.

> Slow down to go faster.

Leap

We're all familiar with Albert Einstein's definition of *insanity*, "doing the same thing over and over and expecting different results." We know it, and we understand it, yet too often we still get stuck in this cycle. We keep going to the same unfulfilling job day after day, hoping something will change and make it better. We keep working hard year after year, hoping someday we'll be recognized and provided a better opportunity. No one is immune to being stuck at varying points along their leadership journey, such as the CEO who keeps implementing the same broken approach and expecting it to eventually yield a different result. We stick with what we know and with what's familiar and wait for external forces to change things for us. It simply doesn't work that way. Sometimes we just have to leap.

I'm going to reintroduce you to John Geraci, who led his CPA firm to a workplace environment equal to a *Field of Dreams* because before he was able to make that possible, he had a bit of recognizing, launching, and leaping to do to get himself unstuck.

It was year twelve of my career with VCC when I understood that I would never make partner there. I also recognized why it was never going to happen. While I had done an excellent job of developing relationships downstream, I had failed to establish meaningful relationships with my senior leadership. Somehow I had missed the need for relationships with the leaders who could support my continued success with the company and potentially within the industry. I was stuck and knew that if I was going to reach my goal of partner, I was going to have to move on.

John knew that if he was going to launch his partnership career, he would need to find a new firm to make that happen. In 2009 he chose to move from a 375-person firm to a 20-person firm.

The premise of the choice was all about knowing that they had got great clients and long-standing relationships but that they lacked the leadership to shift the firm toward a progressive nature, which is where the industry and service organizations in general needed to go. Suddenly, I found myself in a new organization where seeking and developing new relationships from a business development and a referral partner relationship standpoint became important. This was not part of my existing skill set.

I had never done a good job of building external relationships, one, because my previous firm had grown so
quickly it made it really easy for me to get complacent
about new business development and, two, because,
the truth is I wasn't comfortable networking. I always
considered myself more of an intimate relationship
developer. Walking into a room and being assigned one
person to establish a relationship was more my speed.
Walking into a room with the goal of initiating multiple
conversations with people I didn't already have a relationship with was definitely out of my comfort zone.

Could John make the leap required to push himself out of his
comfort zone and do what he needed to do to achieve his vision? The
answer is *Yes Man*.

In 2011 I watched the Jim Carrey movie *Yes Man*. It was
an amazing moment for me because, in the movie, Jim
Carrey constantly says no at work, to family, and to
friends—just no to everyone and everything. It really hit
home for me because that was me. I tended to say no to
everything, even simple things like going out to dinner
to meet our new neighbors. When my wife suggested
it, my response was, "We have friends. Why do we need
more friends? Why do we want to go to dinner with new
people?"

In *Yes Man* Jim Carrey's character goes to a seminar
and commits to saying yes to everything. No matter
what anyone asked him, he was committed to saying
yes. I decided that's what I was going to do. At the time,

I had been networking with an attorney who asked me to meet an individual who was running a purchasing group and needed an accountant who wasn't so black and white. My impulse was to say no, but I had watched *Yes Man* and agreed to meet with him. I walked into the restaurant, thinking, "Hopefully, this won't take long, and I'll be on my way."

The three of us had dinner, and just as I thought it would play out, the attorney and the prospect talked together all night. We were sitting alongside each other at the bar, game seven of the Stanley Cup finals was on, and I wondered, "Why did I say yes to this?"

Their conversation wound down, and the attorney said, "I have to get home. I told my son I would watch game seven with him." The prospect, Tom, invited me to stay and have another drink with him.

All I wanted to do was say "good night" and leave, but I was committed to saying yes to everything, so instead I said, "That'd be great."

I attribute my watching *Yes Man* and my decision to say yes to Tom's invitation to stay and have a drink with him to be the two most influential aspects of my business life.

Tom opened the door to so many connections for me. Committing to saying yes turned me into a social butterfly overnight. Taking advantage of every opportunity Tom presented me unlocked a confidence that allowed me to navigate uncomfortable situations. I had worked with a couple of coaches at my prior firm who were trying to get me comfortable doing these same things, but nothing I tried moved the needle. *Yes Man* made me see that it was all about mindset, about putting ourselves into a certain headspace. When you are open, engaged, and willing, you'll be able to recognize all the opportunities in front of you.

John's leadership leap resulted in not only becoming a partner at LGA but also reaching the rank of managing partner. Under his leadership LGA has risen in the ranks of the *Boston Business Journal's* Largest Accounting Firms from forty-fifth in 2013 to twenty-fourth in 2021.

Keep Your Eye on the Ball

Sometimes we may be ready to take the leap, but the opportunity just doesn't present itself. You can continue doing everything possible to prepare for that moment not knowing when it will come or even if it will come. The decision to stick with the stuckness for a bit or to move on to new possibilities is a personal decision. NFL player Matt Cassel decided to remain stuck on the quarterback bench for several seasons; his patience and focus paid off.

In high school, Matt had his choice of colleges to play football at. He chose USC because as he puts it, "USC was in my own backyard, and I thought I'd be able to play early there." It didn't go exactly as planned. He got the call from the USC coach that the starting QB was going to be Matt Leinart, but the coach assured him that if there were any hiccups, Matt would be in. Not only were there no hiccups for Matt but he also ended up winning the Heisman Trophy. Cassel would remain on the bench.

When asked how he stayed motivated while relegated to the bench, Cassel shares that it required a level of self-motivation. He had to find his own way to deal with the adversity because "Once you start hanging your head and giving in to the frustration, it takes away from your ability to compete at a high level." For Cassel that meant working even harder to be the best QB he could be and to find other opportunities that enabled him to contribute to the team. Those contributions included playing tight end, catching balls in the receiver position, and playing special teams in the Rose Bowl.

Cassel admits he had a level of frustration and disappointment in his junior year of still not being where he envisioned he would be at this point in his football career. So he decided to take a reprieve and play baseball for USC that spring. In his senior year, he had a decision to make: return to baseball or take the opportunity to participate in pro day for the NFL football scouts.

"It was always my dream and my vision to go out for pro day. Physically, I had the tool set. I just didn't have the experience because I didn't play much." His coach discouraged him from participating, telling him, "You know what, Cassel, you might want to think about another profession."

Cassel didn't take his advice. Instead, he kicked it up a gear. "I'm going to go out and train my butt off—that's what I know how to do. I got myself ready. I had an understanding that I could do something else, but if I didn't try it [on pro day], I would always be kicking myself. And thank god I did because it worked out."

Cassel was an unknown that day, but he threw great, and the scouts jumped on him. He was drafted by the Patriots but once again found himself on the bench. He would be backup to none other than Tom Brady. Cassel remained undeterred. Instead of seeing it as a setback, he seized the opportunity to be mentored by an amazing QB.

For three years he watched, listened, and learned. He asked questions, took notes, and worked hard. Herein lies the difference between being stuck because you're comfortable with the familiar and afraid to make the leap and choosing to be in a holding pattern while you continue to hone your skills in preparation for the opportunity you have been dreaming of.

During the first quarter of Cassel's fourth season with the Patriots, Brady was taken off the field with an injury. He was out for the game, and Cassel was in, and he was ready, leading the Patriots to a win that day and an 11–5 record for the season. For more than five years, Cassel kept his head in the game even though he was on the sidelines. He committed to working at the level of a starting quarterback even though he didn't know if he would ever reach that position. Now it had all finally paid off. Because Cassel was ready for the leap when it was put in front of him, his vision became a reality.

Brady returned the following season, but Cassel didn't go back on the bench. In 2009 he was picked up by the Kansas City Chiefs as their *starting* quarterback. The KC franchise was in the process of rebuilding, and he knew he had his work as the leader cut out for him. That first season Cassel started 15 games for the Chiefs, throwing for 2,924 yards and 16 touchdowns. Year 2010 was even better. Cassel threw for 3,116 yards and 27 touchdowns, leading the Chiefs to a 10–6 record and the AFC West win.[17] Matt had a choice: hang his head in disappointment, call himself unlucky for backing up a college Heisman Trophy winner and an NFL MVP, or focus on becoming the best version of himself knowing he would get a chance

---

17 Stephen Ur, "Matt Cassel's Collapse: The Cassel Story," Last Word on Sports, June 1, 2016, https://lastwordonsports.com/2016/06/01/matt-cassels-collapse/.

someday—everyone would agree Matt made the right choice and had a very successful NFL career that young boys dream of.

Overcome

Just as stuckness is an inevitable, recurring aspect of the leadership journey, the same is true of challenges. Sometimes as a leader you are called to help others overcome their barriers to success, and other times as a leader, you must find your own inspiration and strength to overcome the challenges you face. Matt Cassel drew on his own strength and positive mindset to overcome the challenges he faced on the way to attaining his dream, and he is certainly not alone.

Before Amanda Rogers began leaping to new leadership heights in her career, she had a significant personal challenge to overcome. During a lacrosse practice in her senior year in college, Amanda wound up with a serious concussion that not only ended her lacrosse career but also forced her to move back home and basically put her life on hold.

> For a while my memory was poor, and I couldn't read anything, and I couldn't watch anything digital. I had a pity party for myself in the first eight or nine months of recovery. Once I started feeling a bit better, I would sit at Barnes and Noble, listen to audiobooks, and people-watch. One day I walked in and was drawn to a book called *The Power of Now*. I later got the audio version and listened to it.
>
> The premise of the book is that, at its simplest level, the only thing that's real is this moment. Anything we project into the future or the past is simply our projec-

tion. That was a life-changing concept for me. Here I was in this place of wanting to be anywhere else than where I was. Where I wanted to be was back out on the field, completely healed, and playing lacrosse, but that didn't look like that would be happening anytime soon or maybe ever.

I realized that I needed to get into the present moment and be OK here so that I could heal. From that moment when I committed to that notion, my whole world opened up. I now saw my concussion as a unique opportunity to learn outside the scope of what I was learning in college.

Amanda took this time of being in the present to learn about meditation and the power of mindfulness and how to build her brain back in a different way. She embarked on a path of building her own tools to be able to be a leader. Shortly after adopting this new mindset, the right people started showing up in Amanda's life. At the point where she was almost fully healed, an opportunity to get back into the lacrosse world again opened up not as a player but as a coach of a high school team and a founder of a girls' lacrosse program in New Hampshire.

During the five years I was involved with the program, I had an opportunity to really create a vision of what I thought the experience could be like as a student athlete. I wanted to create not only an inclusive community where people really had fun and loved being part of the team and creating memories that lasted a lifetime but also a program that opened opportunities for young girls to play college lacrosse if they wanted to.

Today more than four hundred girls are involved in the program, and so many of them have college commitments to all sorts of schools including Georgetown, Stanford, and University of Virginia.

Amanda didn't just overcome her concussion challenge but she also motivated herself to grow in new ways because of it. Fearless Leadership isn't about overcoming a challenge to get you back to where you were; it's about finding the opportunity in the challenge to grow beyond that point.

It was through Amanda's coaching job that I met her at the sports award dinner and offered her the ten-hour-per-week contracting position.

When I started working for Brendan, my memory still wasn't good. I wrote down everything he asked me to do so that I wouldn't forget. Brendan and the company were moving so quickly, and I had to push myself to adapt just as quickly. I was so hyperfocused on making sure that I was able to achieve the goals set for me that I kind of built this new neural pathway to be more productive.

Amanda developed the mindset that productivity is a choice and that everything comes back to the ultimate vision of "If I feel connected to the work I'm doing or I feel like my work is impactful, I will naturally be more productive."

I believe that there are no accidents and that my concussion was put in my path for a reason. It helped me rewire the neuropathways in my brain to become who I am today.

That's the mindset of a truly Fearless Leader.

What Can We Do Better?

There is no shortage of challenges along our individual leadership paths, and often those challenges require us to inspire our team to look at things in new ways to overcome the obstacles in front of us. Sometimes we can get so stuck in the how-things-have-always-been-done cycle that we can't see the obvious first step in front of us. Tye Kuhlman is not one of those people. Remember Tye from chapter 3, the individual who commanded influence without the leadership title to go with it? One of the qualities that makes Tye a natural influencer is his innate growth mindset, and his innate growth mindset is a primary reason he can overcome any challenge put in front of him.

By now I'm sure you can't help but see the common thread between all Fearless Leaders; they embody and employ all the attributes of a strong leader throughout their lives. My focus here is Tye's ability to overcome challenges, but I can't talk about that without talking about his ability to inspire, influence, and grow. Fearless Leadership is the whole package.

In my experience with Tye, he was always the guy who came to the table with new ideas on how to better serve our customers, and he is also often the one initiating the gathering around the table. He's the one who says, "We got a QBR [quarterly business review] next week. Let's preview it. I've got three ideas I want to share." Tye's mindset of constantly asking, "What can we do better?" was contagious, and each idea he shared stimulated other ideas that people around the table would jump in with, creating a highly collaborative energy. Here's Tye's story of his role in helping his team overcome a significant customer problem.

In my role in the business management office, I was in charge of our largest and most important customer. They were also our unhappiest customer. They were a technology manufacturer, and in our role with them, we were considered what they called a WOB—worst of breed. Our performance was horrible, and they let us know it at the QBRs, telling us just how awful we were, how much better our competitors were, and all of that interspersed with fists pounding on the table. Those QBRs were extremely uncomfortable two-hour sessions where we just took a beating. Within a period of about eight months, we went from worst of breed to best of breed. And we completely changed their attitude about us, and a year and a half later, we became their supplier of the year. It was fun turning that around, something that can't be done without a good team of people around you.

So how did Tye and his team make their least satisfied customer to their most satisfied customer in just eight months? It involved a lot of fact and data collecting and, based on those findings, calling out the shortcomings of their own group and how they were contributing to the poor performance and neglecting to take corrective action.

One of the first steps I took was to require the group who was largely responsible for the performance of the day-in-and-day-out service delivery to be part of the QBR. It just didn't make sense to me that they did not have a presence in those meetings; they were responsible for driving the poor performance, and if we were going to solve the problem, we needed to know why and how that was happening.

They were reluctant to be in the room. They didn't want to hear all the negative feedback our customer threw at us, but we worked through the ego stuff and agreed to look at the facts and data and put a plan together to fix it. The collaboration was successful. And just as I required the team that was responsible for causing the problem to be in the room to hear firsthand the dissatisfaction of our customer, I also made sure that same team, who also fixed the problem, was in the room when we became the best of breed and when we received the supplier of the year award.

Tye knows his role as a leader. In this scenario it wasn't to go to operations and fix it. It was to bring all the essential players together; diffuse the fear, uncertainty, and doubt of his team and customer; facilitate the dialogue that would create positive change; and in the end recognize his team for a job well done.

To lead successfully you have to operate from a principled foundation. How do you self-manage, what are your values and vision, do you lead by example, and are you the same type of person when you're out of the spotlight as you are when you're in it? Then you build on that foundation by inspiring others to want to work alongside you.

Inspiration is an accelerating factor because once you get two or three people on your team with a shared vision and values, it becomes a multiplier. Another important factor of a strong leader is coaching others and the willingness to be coached. You have to support, encourage, and lead others to their potential, and you have to be approachable and humble enough to openly receive the ideas and thoughts that others bring to you. If I have a blind spot, I want the people on my team to tell me what that blind spot is. And finally, show your gratitude and celebrate the wins of your team members.

Pay attention to those you are leading. If they are stumbling, reach out and help them find their way. If you are the one stumbling along your path to Fearless Leadership, seek out the guidance of your mentors to help you find your way or, like Amanda, be open to inspiration, accept what you do and do not have control of, and dig into your courage and strength to find your path forward to overcoming whatever stands in your way.

Grow

Here we look ahead to the future and ask what it takes to create a practice of constant and continuous growth: how can we be better? If you don't have a growth mindset; if you think once you've reached a certain level, you're good with what you know and the skills you have; and if you stop trying to be better, you're immediately getting worse because when everyone around you is continuing to expand their skill set and grow and you're not, you immediately start to fall behind. If you think you've made it, your best days are probably behind you. Reach for positions above your current competencies and lean into the opportunity to grow.

When I landed my first CEO role, my initial reaction was, "Wow, I did it." I had worked hard toward this goal, and then suddenly, I realized, "Holy shit, I am so ill prepared for this." I was bombarded with questions from HR, finance, legal, marketing, sales, operations, and technology, and I was comfortable with only three of the seven. I'd get questions like, "Brendan, we have to update our PTO policy this year. What are your thoughts?" I had zero thoughts about PTO policies.

> Be open to inspiration, accept what you do and do not have control of, and dig into your courage and strength to find your path forward.

Legal would say, "Brendan, we need you to make a decision on three aspects in this legal case. We can do A, B, or C. What's your recommendation?" Again, zero thoughts on the matter; forget about any educated recommendations. I had never sat in a room discussing wrongful termination; I had never contemplated PTO packages for all employees. I realized that if I thought I had to grow before I took this job, that was an understatement. To keep this job, I knew I had to grow times one hundred.

It always amazes me when people don't take advantage of even low-hanging opportunities. One thing we offer every single employee at Merchants Fleet is LearniQ, which means you can go to any one on a list of fifty colleges like USC or MIT and take a microcredential LearniQ, and we'll pay for it. Out of six hundred employees, about three hundred take advantage of it every year. The HR folks are over the moon with that number because it is significantly higher than it used to be, but I'm still shocked that three hundred people didn't find twenty hours during the year to take a free course. As leaders it is our job not just to encourage others to grow but also to exemplify a growth mindset through our intentions and actions. Personally, I take advantage of this program every year and have taken courses on innovation from Columbia, digital marketing from U Penn, fostering diversity from Yale, and neuroscience from MIT, and everyone has access to these. Each time I take one of these, I come out with some "big idea" for the company. In fact, twice I have brought the professors and consultants teaching the courses on campus to work with the entire company. We all have a chance to grow; we just need to remain open minded. So how are you going to grow?

Contagious Leadership

Paul LeBlanc, president of Southern New Hampshire University (SNHU), is an exemplary example of a growth mindset leader who is always looking to do better and to be better. He's a leader who could walk into the worst franchise in the country with ten years of declining revenue and in a year get it to grow 50 percent. Paul is a guy who embraces growth and gets everybody in the room to embrace it along with him. He's really magical about it.

A couple of years ago, Paul asked me to facilitate building their strategic plan, and during one of those planning meetings, we talked about the possibility of developing this great new program. That's when Paul turned to one of the deans and said, "Next week find ten students who are willing to enter this pilot program for free with the agreement that they will provide us structured feedback. In return we'll give them free tuition next year." That was a wow for me. Paul knew if SNHU wanted to create this new program and get a hundred students in it, get a thousand students in it, or get five thousand students in it online, they would need ten students to go through it and provide the school some real data on if and how to move forward.

Paul made it immediately actionable with little room for anyone to counter that it didn't make sense, and that growth mindset empowered his team. Just imagine if you're the person walking out of that meeting, eager to find ten students to give free tuition to so you can develop an exciting new program. That person thinks they can run through a brick wall, right? Paul's magical growth mindset is contagious all the way down to the students who are invited to participate in a cutting-edge pilot program *and* receive free tuition. I've seen Paul inspire this type of leap at least three times in a single session.

Paul likes to joke that he's in a slow-to-innovate industry that likes to push everything to "We'll do that next year." But it's not Paul's innovative ideas that are the key to his success. It's his ability to rise to the challenge of winning the hearts and minds of those who may lack innovation and inspiring them to think big, to think, "Why not?" and to think, "We can do this." As a result people will follow him wherever he leads. People want to do great things for him and with him because they see the great things he is doing for the university. You can start a full-day strategy meeting with Paul at 9:00 a.m., and at 5:00 p.m., I guarantee everyone is going to walk out of that room knowing the organization is better than when they started the day. Paul's leadership isn't just impacting SNHU but it's also challenging the traditional concept of secondary education in the United States and across the globe.

I often say we're the university for people for whom college is not a guarantee. That could be a first-generation college kid whose mom and dad run a little corner store in New England, or it could be a single mom across the country who's holding down a full-time job and has a couple of kids and is now trying to go back and finish her college degree because she has an opportunity in her company if she could just get that diploma, or it could be an international student whose family has pooled all of their resources to give their child an opportunity to come to America to study, knowing that when they come back home, that college degree could change the direction of not just that student's life but also the lives of everyone in their family. We're creating an educational system that is accessible to people all around the world.

SNHU is in the forefront of bringing competency-based programming to higher education.

Our competency-based program is the first of its kind to be approved in the United States, and it really moves away from the way we traditionally think about education, which is we take this course, then this course, then this course, and typically, they're 3 credits each. And when we accumulate 60 credits, we earn an associate degree. And when we have 120 credits, we earn a bachelor's degree. At SNHU we recognized that credit hours are really good at telling the world how long you sat, but they don't really say much about how much you know, so we instead built a degree program that's based on competencies.

There are 120 competencies for our associate degree and 244 for our bachelor's degree. We group the competencies, so for example, there's a set of communications competencies, quantitative reasoning competencies, and ethics and critical thinking competencies. The student moves through those competencies by doing projects that demonstrate mastery. Let's say you are an adult who's been working the family business for twenty years, and you've been the bookkeeper, and you look at those math competencies and know you already have the knowledge and skills in that area; why would we make you sit through sixteen weeks of college math? Let's instead give you a project that demonstrates your mastery. Employers love it because they can understand how the competencies relate to the positions they are needing to fill.

We live in an age when employers are increasingly skeptical about the ability of higher ed to produce workforce-ready graduates. There's one famous study by Gallup that indicates 93 percent of university provosts believe their graduates are ready for work on day one, and only 8 percent of employers believe that. That's a huge gap. SNHU is closing that gap with our competency-based program.

I can't even begin to calculate the exponential impact of Paul's visionary leadership. He makes us all want to grow with him and see where it takes us. Paul's visionary and energetic leadership is positively contagious.

It's Never Too Late to Grow

I'm starting this one out with a story about a guy who was so stuck in his way of doing things for so long that nobody in the company thought it was possible for him to make the changes necessary for him to continue working there. No one thought he was capable of growing in new ways. Phil was a sales savant, the proverbial "could sell ice to the Eskimos" kind of guy. He was our number-two salesperson out of 1,200. He sold seventy-five million a year, and his clients absolutely loved him, so when the notice that he was going to be let go came across my desk, I immediately said, "Time out, what's going on here?"

I talked to everyone except his direct manager. I learned that everyone in the company hated working with him—the operations team, the customer service team, everyone. He was a total jerk to everyone in the office. All he cared about was getting the proposal to the customer and making the sale, and he didn't care that he mowed everyone down in the process. This had been going on for years, and everyone had had enough. They were right, no one should be treated the way Phil had been treating all of them, but I couldn't help but wonder whether Phil even recognized what he was doing. He was several levels of supervision below me, but I decided it was worth me flying out to have a brutally honest conversation with him.

I take him out to dinner and tell him straight out, "They're going to fire you."

"What? That's bullshit. You guys can't do that. I'm one of the company's best salespeople," said Phil.

"No one will ever debate how great a salesperson you are. Externally, you're a magician. I've been on calls with you. I've seen you with your clients. You are the most likable guy. You're a gentleman. You're gracious. You're an incredible listener. But in the office, you're a devil. You tell everyone how stupid they are. All you care about is the client. And you run everybody over," I said.

"But," he argued, "I'm not doing that for me. I'm doing that for the client."

"When no one in the company wants to help you make that sale, you're no longer doing it for the client. It takes thirty people in the company to help you create a proposal and close the sale, but right now there isn't even one person in the company who is willing to help you. You have been voted off the island."

He was devastated. He only saw himself as a superstar producer and a hero to our customers. On his own he wasn't able to recognize that that wasn't enough. "What can I do?" he asked. "I love this company. I love what I do. I'll do anything to make it right. Just name it, and I'll make it happen tonight."

"Well, you can't just make it tonight because what I need is external Phil to also be internal Phil. You can't continue to be this amazing leader externally and a jerk of a manager internally. And that's what you're doing. You need to be the same amazing leader with your internal team that you are with your customers."

"But what if we miss a deadline?" he asked.

"People will surprise you, Phil. They won't miss the deadline. You've got a team of good people who deserve to be treated with respect and appreciation."

We strategized how he could best systemically make the change. This wasn't a "bring in doughnuts for the team" type of solution; this required personal growth on Phil's part. He intentionally had to be external Phil with everyone. He did it. He humbled himself, and he grew into an amazing leader with his team. That growth was able to occur because he recognized his need for change, he strategized how to best launch his new internal approach, and then he took the leap to trust that his team would still meet deadlines with the new internal Phil.

This growth process required Phil to have humility, courage, EQ, and influence. I could list several more attributes of a Fearless Leader, but my point is Fearless Leadership requires you to, at varying points in your journey, draw on all of the attributes we have talked about. Fearless Leadership is not linear or a "one approach fits all." It is an intentional development of the required attributes and an intentional and ongoing engagement of those attributes.

I am so proud of what Phil was able to accomplish, but more importantly, he is a case study and reminder to all of us that we have what it takes inside us; we just have to harness the power within ourselves with good intentions and learn each day how to channel our fearlessness.

Just Be

We've covered a lot of ground, and you're still with me! That tells me that you are ready to embark on the inaugural launch of your Fearless Leadership journey, or you are already a Fearless Leader ready to take it to the next level. Either way I am excited for you and what your leadership future holds for you and, even more importantly, the impact you can have on those around you.

We all begin and grow in our Fearless Leadership journey at different moments in our career and in our life.

Emerging leaders like Andi Shaughnessy and Danielle Carter were pushed into their leadership position due to circumstances, wanted to be successful, and not only sought out help from other successful leaders but also listened to their advice *and* took action on it. They have emerged as truly Fearless Leaders who are always challenging themselves to get better.

Stuck leaders like John Cail was stuck in a risk-adverse mindset of leading, a mindset that impeded the company's exponential growth opportunities. It took sitting with the team of people he supervised, who believed that together they could jump-start a new business in a big way, to open his mind to a fearless way of leading. Once unstuck, John embraced the Fearless Leader mindset, leading the charge to go from a three-hundred- to three-thousand-fleet commitment in ninety days with no plan or safety net in place.

Challenged leaders like Zak Brown, as a seasoned Fearless Leader, jumped at the opportunity to take on the significant and long-term challenges of McLaren Racing and against significant odds continues to overcome the challenges put before him, setting his team on a winning track.

Get-better leaders like Amanda Rogers, even in her early days leading her fellow classmates on the lacrosse field, was always driven to learn, improve, and simply be a better leader. She was a Fearless Leader who reframed her extreme health setback into an opportunity to build herself back better than before.

If there is one thing that these different leaders confirm, it's that Fearless Leadership is not a one-size-fits-all approach or a linear trajectory. Being a Fearless Leader requires you to commit to

- being fearless in your efforts to overcome fear, doubt, and uncertainty not just in yourself but also in those you lead;
- being a leader every single day and sharing the gift with others;
- being good by embodying and modeling the Fearless Leadership attributes of strength, courage, faith, service, humility, and leadership;
- being impactful through the best practices of communicating a clear vision, setting challenging and attainable goals, and establishing a simple system to produce results;
- being collaborative with all stakeholders, employees, investors, customers, and vendors in a meaningful way by intentionally and authentically developing and continually improving your brand, relationships, communication, EQ, and influence;

- being legendary by leading, coaching, mentoring, and culti-vating emerging, stuck, challenged, and get-better leaders and giving them the gift of Fearless Leadership; and
- beginning the next phase of your Fearless Leadership journey by recognizing the moments along the way when you need to launch, leap, and overcome and never ever stop growing as a person, professional, and leader.

The Fearless Leadership approach that I have laid out for you in *The FUD Factor: Overcoming Fear, Uncertainty, and Doubt to Achieve the Impossible* has cultivated, empowered, and inspired thousands of people to grow as a Fearless Leader. I know it can do the same for you.

Just be yourself. Be authentic. And stretch yourself in the directions that instill your values and fuel your passions.

Fearless Leadership

is a daily decision, which is why the journey doesn't stop here at the end of this book. Continue the conversation with me on the following channels, where you can find lots of free content including tips, programs, podcasts, articles, and information on my speaking engagements:

Facebook, Instagram, Twitter, and LinkedIn: **@bpkfearless**
Brendanpkeegan.com
fearless@brendanpkeegan.com
https://forbesbooksaudio.com/shows/fearless-leadership/

About the Author

Brendan P. Keegan is a capitalist, opportunist, philanthropist, inclusionist, and thought leader. He is a six-time president and CEO and author of *The FUD Factor*, *Be Fearless*, and *Fearlessly 4WARD*. He's a world-renowned expert and award-winning executive in the areas of market disruption, business transformation, hypergrowth, and leadership. He has published over two hundred articles on strategy, technology, leadership, and business and currently is a monthly editorial contributor for *Fast Company*, *Inc.* magazine, Fox News Digital, *Entrepreneur*, and *Newsweek*. Brendan has raised over $5 billion of capital and returned over $10 billion to investors through his Fearless Leadership approach to business. He has previously been named the World's Most Innovative CEO and recognized as a Top 10 Global Innovative Company by *Fast Company* and Best Managed Company by Deloitte. Brendan received his bachelor's from Rensselaer Polytechnic Institute and his MBA from George Washington University. Brendan is married to his best friend, Dana, and they have raised two fearless kids, Kaylie and Patrick.